M000114289

Conquering Your Kitchen

Annemarie Rossi

Copyright © 2014 by Angela England Media

All rights reserved. This book or any portion thereof may not be reproduced or used in any manner whatsoever without the express written permission of the publisher except for the use of brief quotations in a book review.
Printed in the United States of America

First Printing, 2014

ISBN-13: 9780692237533

Angela England Media
4019 W. Hwy 70 #252
Durant, OK 74701

www.angelaenglandmedia.com

Ordering Information:
Quantity sales. Special discounts are available on quantity purchases by corporations, associations, and others. For details, contact the publisher at the address above.

Printed in the United States of America

FOREWORD

"Help! My mother never taught me how to cook!" The call that was sent across my mother's group email list became the impetus for the initial creation of Untrained Housewife. The entire community, media company, and amazing group of authors developed out of my desire to help empower women. To bring in amazing women with something valuable to share, then highlight their voice in the community. And this book serves to culminate five years of effort into one of the most helpful and useable works we've created to date.

The Untrained Housewife community has not only taught me, but it has also introduced me to some amazing, brilliant, and caring people. Annemarie is one of those women.

From the very first post she shared on Untrained Housewife, it was clear that she not only had something valuable to share, but she has the ability to share in a way that is encouraging and uplifting. I am so excited to bring this book to you and to highlight, once again, a voice from our community that has something empowering to share.

From the start of Untrained Housewife's evolution, I felt an anger at the sense of overwhelm that women were experiencing, and that drove me. And I still have a desire to ease that feeling. It doesn't make sense to me that we have an entire generation of women who are brilliant! Savvy! Educated! Capable! Yet they feel defeated by their kitchen cupboards every evening at 4 pm.

This book is the ultimate solution to that feeling, and if you implement the time-tested wisdom Annemarie shares here, you'll not have to experience that feeling again. Her simple techniques will help you eat healthier, become more confident, and conquer the feeling of inability that made me so angry all those years ago. I'm ever grateful to Annemarie for bringing my vision to life.

Angela England
Founder, Untrained Housewife and Homestead Bloggers Network
http://untrainedhousewife.com
http://homesteadbloggersnetwork.com

DEDICATION

I dedicate this book to my wonderful family. Thank you, Rick, Luke, and Julia, for encouraging me, for being my taste-testers, and for signing on to this switch to homemade food. You motivate me to be my best self, and I feel beyond blessed to have you for my family.

TABLE OF CONTENTS

APPENDIX
1. Basic Cooking Terms
2. Kitchen Measurement Conversion Chart
3. Dirty Dozen/Clean Fifteen Produce Guide
4. Where to Store Produce
5. Other Resources
6. Make-Ahead Meals

ACKNOWLEDGMENTS

My mom taught me how to cook a handful of things, including apple pie and baked potatoes. But more importantly, she taught me how to be kind and generous, how to persevere, and how to write. She always encouraged my sense of wonder. My dad ingrained in me the message that I was incredibly capable, and that I could do anything I wanted. My parents shaped me into who I've become, and I'm grateful.

My husband, Rick, comes from a family of DIYers. When I married into this family, I caught the spirit. I thank Monica and Frank for instilling a sense of "I can do this myself" in their son. It has led to many projects and creations that I couldn't have ever imagined.

Angela England recognized this book in me before I knew it was there. She had faith in me, sight unseen, and I'm so grateful for that. Brannan Sirratt has been a fantastic editor, taking care of the details behind the scenes. It was so nice to write without worrying about whether I was missing a comma somewhere.

Our recipe testers helped to insure the quality and clarity of all the recipes in this book. I'm grateful to all of them for taking a stab at these recipes and giving their honest feedback. They are Rachel Arsenault, Becca Carroll, Chara, Andrea Fabry, Jaye Anne Gallagher, Heather Jackson, Karen Lynn, Tammy Nelson, Heidi Ramsey, Stephanie Redin, Jo Rellime, Kathryn Robles, Carissa Rogers, Angi Schneider, Kelly Smith, Sreevalli, Erin Scholtens Ter Beest, Kathleen Yorba, and Tessa Zundel.

It wasn't until the last word of this book was written that I had actually conquered my own kitchen. The best way to learn how to do something is to teach it to someone else. So I thank you for opening up this book and entering into the process of conquering *your* kitchen. I hope this book will help you to feel stronger, more confident, and more competent in feeding your families and yourself the way you all deserve to be fed.

INTRODUCTION

I love food. As a scrawny little girl, I loved steak and green beans and potatoes. I asked my mom to make Brussels sprouts for dinner. But I didn't like tomatoes or anything that touched or came near tomatoes. No pizza, no pasta sauce, no ketchup. I was a quirky little eater, and my palate was narrow. I ate hamburgers without a roll, and I liked peanut butter sandwiches without jelly. I loved chocolate chip cookies and pastries.

Then I grew up and moved out on my own. I had so much to learn. The first thing I figured out was how to make chocolate chip cookies. I made batch after batch, and I mastered that Toll House recipe. Brownies came soon after. Once I got over my tomato thing, I would boil pasta and pour jarred sauce on it for dinner. Then I'd make something yummy for dessert, something from scratch.

I always wanted to eat healthy (plus dessert, of course). It took me many years to learn what healthy really meant, though. I wasn't concerned with dieting or losing weight, but I wanted to take care of my body. For years in early adulthood, I ate a jam-filled cereal bar every day for a snack. It had "grain" in the title, so I thought it must be healthy. I'll never forget the day I actually read the ingredient label on a box of those bars. I had been eating the nutritional equivalent of a donut. Every day. For years. I had no idea.

Once I became a mother, the whole game changed. Now I was responsible for the food that other people would eat. Over the years, I've learned the importance of making our food from scratch - not just the cookies and brownies, but the regular food too. When my kids were younger, I served plenty of processed food. And every time a cold or stomach bug passed through their school, they'd bring it home. My husband or I would usually pick it up, too. At least six times a year, we'd be fighting off the latest virus.

Then I tried something. I stopped buying packaged foods and started making just about everything from scratch. The prepared foods that I did buy had short ingredient lists with things I would cook with at home. We moved to a whole foods diet, and the results were beyond what I could have imagined. We stopped getting sick. My son's complaints of stomach aches gradually disappeared. I started sleeping better, and my seasonal allergies went away completely. After years of being regularly congested with colds and allergies, I could breathe again.

I was so happy to find a way to keep my family healthy. But, man, cooking everything from scratch can be quite a task.

Three meals a day, seven days a week, 365 days a year. The need for food never takes a break. Decide what to eat, shop for the food, prepare the food, eat, clean up, repeat. It's no wonder many people turn to takeout windows and pre-packaged meals to deal with this never-ending cycle. But the Standard American Diet is making people unhealthy, overweight, and dissatisfied with their reality. It doesn't have to be this way.

There *is* a better way, and I'm going to walk you through it. There are many details to learn, but you can master a healthy, homemade kitchen. With the right setup and strategy, you can embrace your kitchen and efficiently feed your family nutritious, affordable food. Maybe you don't want to make *all* your food from scratch, but you're ready to dip your toe in the water. This book will give you lots of ideas to get you started. If you're not sure where to begin, I recommend chocolate chip cookies (p. 203). Even if you mess up, they'll still be delicious.

Conquering your kitchen is within reach. You just need the skills and confidence to do it. It's not rocket science, but it does take dedication, experimentation, and lots of taste tests. You may even find that you actually enjoy cooking food from scratch. If not, at least you'll enjoy eating it, and so will your family.

PART ONE
GET ORGANIZED

In Part One, we look at the behind-the-scenes skills that the home cook should master in order to maintain an efficient kitchen. Good organization is the essential first step toward taking ownership of your kitchen. Learning how to meal plan is the next tool you'll need in order to save time, money, and sanity. Savvy grocery shopping is the final piece that will help you bring together everything you need to get the job done in the kitchen.

CONQUERING YOUR KITCHEN

19

Chapter One
Setting the Stage for Kitchen Success

The kitchen is the heart of the home. This casual, functional room is more than just a place to cook. Food draws us in, but then we stay. We chat about our days and share silly jokes. We eat snacks and do homework and make muffins together. Life slows down a bit at dinnertime, when we sit around the table for a shared meal. This is when I hear about my children's recess antics and my husband's work stories. Distractions like phones and computers are set aside, and I can look around the dinner table at the faces of the people I love most. The kitchen is a place of connection, and it should be set up in a way that facilitates that connection.

Even the most organized kitchen can turn into a big mess if it isn't properly maintained. This is the one room in the house where you can't arrange everything once and expect it to stay that way. Food comes and goes from the cabinets and refrigerator, and new items are regularly introduced to the environment. Every new bag of rice and set of storage containers needs to land somewhere in the kitchen. Without a system, it's impossible to control all of the "stuff" that comes into this room. In this chapter, you'll learn how to manage this essential space.

Organization

Many families are now embracing a homemade food lifestyle. In order to do this efficiently, an organized kitchen is a must. You might be looking at a tiny galley kitchen in a studio apartment. Perhaps you have a spacious, eat-in kitchen with loads of cabinet and counter space. Or maybe you're like me. I work out of an average-sized kitchen that could use a broom closet and more pantry space. Some of my kitchen-related items – including a wok, a fondue set, paper towels, and extra flour – are stashed away in corners of the basement and a living room closet. We work with what we've got, and we have to be creative with organization and storage.

LAY OUT YOUR KITCHEN. Where you keep things in your kitchen can make a big difference. For example, in our old kitchen, my husband and I were frustrated by the placement of the garbage bin. Because of the room layout, the only place we could put a large trash bin was at the end of a long counter. Every time we wanted to throw something away, we had to walk across the room. This wasn't a big deal in the grand scheme of things, but it was enough to irritate us several times a day. When we reworked the kitchen layout, we moved the trash to a pull-out drawer in the island right in the middle of the kitchen. It was so nice to eliminate that walk across the room.

The kitchen triangle is based on the three points of the sink, the refrigerator, and the oven. This is your most traveled kitchen area.

Most kitchens are designed with a triangle setup based on three key points – the sink, the fridge, and the oven – because they are the most utilized appliances in the kitchen. In an ideal kitchen, the number of steps between the points in this triangle is minimal. This is your kitchen's "prime real estate," and you should place your most frequently used tools and food items within this zone. Cabinets outside this area in your kitchen should contain items that you use less frequently. If you have a dishwasher, you'll want to keep plates, glasses, and silverware in cabinets close to it. This will speed up the emptying process.

When my children became old enough to get themselves a snack, I decided it was time for me to turn over the reins to them. I rearranged some cabinets and drawers so that they would be able to independently get a bowl, a cup, an apple, and a scoop of popcorn without my participation. I moved their plastic plates and cups into a low drawer that they could reach. I set up a low shelf in our small pantry cabinet stocked with healthy snacks that they were allowed to eat whenever they were hungry. The fruit bowl got a prime location in the middle of the island. I put a folding stepstool in the cabinet under the sink that they could grab when it was time to wash their hands. It's never too early to start training kids to take care of themselves, and I was more than happy to delegate the snack process to their capable little hands.

Ten Tools for the Triangle

Keep the tools you use the most in the epicenter of your kitchen. You don't want to have to walk across the room every time you need one of these essentials:

1. Chopping knives
2. Cutting boards
3. Measuring spoons
4. Measuring cups
5. Mixing bowls
6. High-traffic pots and pans
7. Pot holders
8. Wooden spoons
9. Food processor, blender, or electric mixer
10. Storage containers

Over time, your kitchen organization needs may change. I suggest going through your cabinets and drawers to evaluate everything that's in them. For the things inside the kitchen work triangle, ask yourself if you use each item frequently enough to warrant such prime real estate. Does that lemon zester really need to be front and center? Are there a couple of pots in your pot drawer that you rarely use? If so, find a new place for them.

My kitchen has cabinets that go all the way to the ceiling. In one of these high cabinets, I have a container of rarely used gadgets, like my cherry pitter and cookie cutters. I don't want to relegate them to the basement, but they don't need to be in my prime real estate gadget drawer, either. By the same token, if you're constantly walking across the kitchen to get something that you use daily, find in place in the epicenter where you can access it more easily.

REFRIGERATOR AND FREEZER. A well-organized refrigerator will help save you money. I get frustrated when something goes bad in the fridge and I have to throw it away. The only time this happens is when we ignore it for days on end. Thankfully, there are strategies you can use to avoid this unpleasant result and keep on top of what's in your refrigerator.

A refrigerator works best when it's fairly full. Keep produce in the crisper drawer because the humidity level in the main compartment will hasten the spoiling process. The temperature is highest on the door shelves, so don't keep your milk there or it could turn sour more quickly. For leftovers, use clear, airtight containers so you can see what's inside without opening them. I like Pyrex glass containers with rubber tops. These containers are great because they can go from freezer to fridge to oven to dishwasher. The added benefit of clear containers is that you don't have to listen to people asking you what there is to eat. They can open the fridge and take a look for themselves.

After an item has sat in the refrigerator for a few days, find a way to use it or put it in the freezer. Even perishables like kale or scallions can be used up by putting them into quiche or soup. Set aside a few minutes twice a week to evaluate what's in your refrigerator and find a way to move it through your meal plan. This beats throwing away rotten food any day.

Tip for Preserving Berries

Berries don't last long in the refrigerator before they start to get mushy or moldy. To extend their shelf life, try this trick when you get home from the grocery store or farmers' market. Line a large, shallow storage container with a paper towel. Discard any damaged berries, and place the rest in the container in a single layer. Don't wash the berries until you're ready to use them. This will keep them looking pretty for a few extra days.

Your freezer is an essential tool for backup food. Keep a list of what's in there so you don't have to dig every time you're looking for something. When dealing with freezer storage, it's important to label everything. I use freezer tape and a Sharpie, but masking tape works well, too. Jot down the date, the item name, and the quantity every time you freeze something. You may think you'll remember all the details about that chili or pumpkin purée, but things can easily get lost and forgotten in the abyss of a freezer.

Organize your freezer in a way that makes sense to you. We have a French door refrigerator with a bottom drawer freezer. I keep prepared, homemade foods that are ready to eat in one section. Single ingredients like chopped squash, diced onions, and berries are in another section. Items that turn over more frequently or need to be grabbed easily go in the top drawer section.

Having a second freezer is a luxury we lived without for many years. But we recently got a new fridge, so we put the old one in the basement. I love having this overflow freezer for stocking up. I use it for loaves of bread, homemade chicken broth, meat, and other items that I don't need to access quickly on a regular basis.

Keep An Ice Tray Handy

Keep a couple of ice cube trays on hand. You can use them to freeze single servings of things like lemon juice, pesto, and cranberry sauce. After you freeze them, remove the cubes from the trays and transfer them to a clear, labeled, airtight container.

CABINET STORAGE. In order to keep groceries affordable, it's nice to be able to stock up on items when they're on sale. This requires ample cabinet space, though. I like to keep one package of each item I use regularly in my prime real estate zone, and then I have at least one backup stored in the outskirts. With this setup, I rarely run out of things, because each item goes on the grocery list as soon as I open the backup.

Organized cabinets will help keep your kitchen running efficiently.

Think about what you use most, then prioritize its placement in your kitchen. I love to bake, so I keep my baking supplies in the epicenter of my kitchen. Plates, glasses, silverware, pots, and the trash are also in this prime real estate zone. Things like canned tomatoes, salsa, pasta, and nuts go in a small pantry cabinet at the end of my kitchen. I don't need these things every day, so I don't mind taking a walk across the room when I need one of them.

In addition to our kitchen cabinets, we converted our living room coat closet into an overflow pantry. This allows me to stock up on flour, paper towels, cereal, and other items that wouldn't fit in our kitchen cabinets. It's nice to know that there's a spot in our main living space to accommodate these extras. If your kitchen is short on cabinet space, look around at your closets and see if you can get creative about expanding your pantry capacity.

Within each cabinet, it's a good idea to use baskets and other storage systems to keep things neat and organized. If your spices are gathered in one spot on a spice rack, the space will feel much less chaotic than if the spices are piled on top of each other in a jumbled mess. Pots and pans can be neatly nested inside each other, and onions and potatoes can be placed in baskets in a drawer or cabinet. Investing in racks and containers that make sense for your space is one of the best things you can do to set up a successful kitchen.

Equipment

There are so many kitchen gadgets and appliances out there today that can help make cooking easy and fun. But in order to keep your kitchen running efficiently, you can't buy them all. That donut maker may look really tempting, but think twice before you buy it. If you really want donuts, you could buy a small donut pan that would fit nicely in the drawer on the bottom of your stove. Kitchen gadget impulse purchases are the enemy of an organized kitchen, so think about it carefully before you buy.

Some kitchen tools are extremely helpful for a homemade food lifestyle. Yes, you could get by without them, but food prep would be more stressful. If you're just starting out, these are the things I recommend you get first.

CUTTING SUPPLIES. A home cook needs a collection of good knives. A large *chef's knife* will take care of your chopping needs. A *small paring knife* is useful for more precise cutting. *Serrated knives* are great for cutting bread or meat without ripping them into pieces. A *vegetable peeler* is a must-have tool, unless you don't mind using your paring knife to peel carrots and other produce. I like to have several *cutting boards*, including wooden and dishwasher-safe for when you're cutting garlic or raw meat.

Food Safety Caution

If you don't clean up properly after working with raw meat, you run the risk of exposing your family to food poisoning. Anything that touches raw meat, including cutting boards, knives, and your hands, must be washed thoroughly after each exposure. Wash these kitchen tools with hot, soapy water each time you use them. To play it safe, designate one cutting board for raw meat and don't cut vegetables using the same board.

MIXING SUPPLIES. Every kitchen needs several different sizes of mixing bowls. For storage purposes, it's nice to have a set of *nesting mixing bowls* that can store inside each other. A few *wooden spoons* and *silicone scrapers* should be close at hand for your mixing needs. Both *metal and non-stick spatulas* are useful for flipping different types of food. A *whisk* is also necessary for many recipes.

Nesting bowls store efficiently because they neatly stack inside one another.

BAKEWARE. It's annoying to find a delicious recipe only to discover that the recipe calls for a baking dish in a size you don't have. The most common pan sizes in recipes are *9 by 13 inches* and *8 inches square.* I recommend *glass or ceramic pans* in each of these sizes. It's good to have at least *two cookie sheets* so you can move cookie batches efficiently through the oven. A standard *muffin pan* is a great resource as well, and you won't want to be without a *9-inch pie dish.*

STOVETOP COOKWARE. There are many types of high-quality cookware for the stovetop. *Stainless steel* and *cast iron pans* in several sizes will set you up well. I have 8-inch and 12-inch cast iron skillets that I use almost daily. Recipes often call for a small, medium, or large pot, so you'll want all three sizes. Stainless steel pots or cast-iron *Dutch ovens* work well here. I don't recommend Teflon or aluminum pans. These contain chemicals that can transfer to your food during cooking. You can always put a little oil at the bottom of a cast-iron or stainless steel pan to keep things from sticking.

Caring for Cast Iron Pans

Cast iron pans require a little maintenance to keep them working properly. To season a cast iron pan, heat the pan to a high temperature and add a very thin layer of coconut oil (or other oil with a high smoke point). When the pan cools down, wipe the oil all around the interior of the pan to coat evenly and remove any excess oil. You'll need to regularly season your cast iron pans to keep their non-stick surface working effectively.

SMALL APPLIANCES. You could get by without any of these small appliances, but they do make food preparation much easier. A *food processor, blender,* and *electric mixer* are all very useful. If you don't have money or space for all three, a good quality food processor or blender will cover most of your needs. A *hand-held electric mixer* is an affordable alternative to a large stand mixer like a KitchenAid. Also, a *hand-held immersion blender* is a useful tool for puréeing soups.

There are a few other small appliances that I use all the time. My *toaster* gets a workout several times a week. We have an *electric griddle* that we use on the weekend to make pancakes. The *slow cooker* is a great resource for especially busy days. And popcorn is my favorite whole grain snack, so my *air popper* gets used quite frequently. If your space is limited, though, you can always pop popcorn in a big pan on the stovetop.

FOOD STORAGE CONTAINERS. I can't stress this enough. Having a big supply of high-quality food storage containers is essential for an organized kitchen full of homemade food. Having leftovers in the fridge and a backup food supply in the freezer is vital if you want to stay sane as a home cook. I love the sturdy Pyrex *glass storage containers* with rubber lids. *Mason jars* are also great for food storage. *Zipper bags* and *aluminum foil* are good to keep on hand, although I try to use them sparingly to minimize our household waste. *Silicone lids* are a great non-disposable alternative to foil for covering bowls and other containers in the fridge or oven.

Warning – Plastic Storage Containers

Many people are concerned about plastic storage containers because chemicals from the plastic can leach into the food. Plastic containers with recycling numbers 3 or 7 likely contain substances that can pose health risks, especially to children. Even if you're using safer plastic storage containers (numbers 2, 4, and 5), never heat food in these containers.

HANDHELD HELPERS. In many recipes, measuring is overrated. You can usually estimate quantities and still come out with a great dish. However, when you're just getting started in the kitchen or cooking something for the first time, it's nice to be able to use precise measurements. *Glass measuring cups* are used to measure liquid ingredients. *Metal measuring cups* are for dry ingredients like flour.

A set of *measuring spoons* is important for baking, where you really do want to use the right amount of salt or baking powder. I keep a plastic *tablespoon measuring cup* on hand, too. This handy tool measures up to a quarter cup, or four tablespoons. It's a standing cup, which makes it easier to measure out tablespoons of liquid ingredients like oil or maple syrup.

There are several other handheld kitchen devices that can be very helpful. A *can opener* is a must-have gadget, and a *microplane* is a helpful tool that can be used to zest a lemon or purée a clove of garlic. If you don't have a food processor with a grater attachment, you'll want a *handheld grater* to grate cheese or vegetables. I like to drink lemon water daily, and my *citrus juicer* gets more juice out of the lemon than I would get squeezing it with my hand. A *scale* is a handy tool if you're following a recipe that measures ingredients by weight. And finally, you'll want to have a *timer* (or two) to keep track of everything.

Food to Keep on Hand

FLOUR. White whole wheat flour is my favorite flour for most baking. This is a whole grain product, but it's a little lighter and milder in flavor than traditional whole wheat flour. All-purpose white flour has less nutritional value than whole wheat flour because the germ and bran are stripped away, leaving only the less nutritious endosperm. Whole wheat flour contains more fiber and vitamins than white flour, as well as better blood sugar regulation. As a less-processed product, it's a better choice than all-purpose flour for most baking.

Some people find whole wheat products to be too dense. If you're just starting out with whole grains, you may want to use half white flour and half whole wheat flour in your baking recipes. White flour does have a higher gluten content, which is what makes breads and cakes come out light and fluffy. As you get used to baking with whole wheat flour, over time you can gradually cut back on the all-purpose white flour and increase the amount of whole grain flour.

If you don't tolerate gluten, you can enjoy baked goods by using gluten-free flour. There are many recipes available that use almond flour, coconut flour, and oat flour. I use a simple homemade gluten-free flour mix for some of my baking (p. 219). Rather than depending solely on wheat flour, I like to mix up the grains that my family eats.

RISING AGENTS. Baking powder, baking soda, and yeast are needed in recipes that rise while baking. Again, there are several options at the store. Aluminum-free baking powder is your best choice because there may be health risks associated with consuming aluminum. Baking soda is great to have on hand for lots of reasons besides baking. Your refrigerator will smell better if you keep an open box of baking soda in there to absorb odors. It can also be used as a household cleaner.

SWEETENERS. Many dessert recipes call for highly processed white sugar. I keep organic sugar on hand for occasional use, but my favorite sweeteners to use are maple syrup and honey. These are the least processed forms of sugar, so they're closest to their natural source. Unlike white sugar, maple syrup contains trace minerals such as zinc and manganese. Honey has health benefits, too, including antibacterial and anti-inflammatory properties. Many people find it to be a more effective cough suppressant than over-the-counter cough medicine. I love both of these flavors, so I use maple syrup and honey often in my kitchen.

SPICES AND SEASONINGS. A well-stocked spice cabinet is an important resource for a home cook. Many recipes call for salt, and a walk down the baking aisle at the grocery store will show you that there are several different types of salt to consider. Simple table salt works in most recipes, but it's highly processed. Sea salt that has a colored tint is a better option. Sea salt contains beneficial minerals, and it's derived from the evaporation of seawater. Soy sauce and coconut aminos are other options for adding a salty flavor to a recipe.

Vanilla extract is one of the best flavor enhancers out there. By adding extra vanilla extract to a recipe, you can often cut back on the amount of sugar needed because the vanilla imparts such a rich flavor. Vanilla can be fairly expensive to buy, but it's simple to make your own (p. 218). Homemade vanilla extract costs about five times less than the store-bought version at a typical grocery store, so it makes sense to keep a homemade batch on hand.

I stock lots of spices in my spice cabinet to help flavor my recipes. Cinnamon, chili powder, smoked paprika, and cocoa powder get the most use in my kitchen. I use some other spices less frequently, including cumin, black pepper, ground ginger, parsley, oregano, basil, bay leaves, and curry powder.

Cabinet-Organization Tip

I recommend emptying out all your cabinets once every year. Wipe down the shelves and assess the items that you've removed. Check expiration dates, and also see if there's anything that you don't expect to use any time soon. Toss whatever needs to be tossed, and re-organize what you have left. You'll love having a nice, clean setup inside those cabinets.

COOKING FATS. For many years, popular nutrition advice suggested that eating foods with a high fat content made people fat. I don't agree with this. Research indicates that eating lots of highly processed, sugar-filled food is what makes people overweight. Approximately 25 percent of the average adult's diet should come from fats in order to maintain good health. Essential organs like the heart and the brain need fat to function properly. The three fats I use regularly for cooking are coconut oil, olive oil, and butter. These are less processed than other oils, and they have significant health benefits. Highly refined oils like vegetable and canola oil contain toxins as a result of being processed with high heat, so I avoid them.

DAIRY PRODUCTS. Milk, yogurt, butter, and cheese are great to have in your fridge at all times. I recommend the least processed versions, which are whole milk, full-fat yogurt, real butter, and full-fat cheese without food coloring. Yogurt is a great source of beneficial bacteria for your gut, and it's super easy to make yourself (p. 213). If you're dealing with a dairy sensitivity, many non-dairy milks are available. Unsweetened versions are best, and you should read ingredient labels to make sure you can pronounce what you're drinking.

EGGS. You can get a headache just looking at all the different egg options in the grocery store. From "Grade A" to "Cage-Free" to "Organic," it's hard to know where to focus. The best quality eggs you can buy come from backyard chickens or a local farm. Ideally, the chickens are able to wander freely around a pasture, forage for food, and see daylight every day.

If you have backyard chickens, you're lucky and I envy you. If not, try to find a reliable source of eggs at a local farm or farmers' market. Of course, most of us need to grab a dozen eggs at the grocery store on occasion. I recommend choosing cage-free, organic eggs if you can afford them. Chapter Four includes more information about eggs and how to use them.

PANTRY ITEMS. There are several items that I like to keep stocked in my pantry. With each of these items, I can make many different recipes. Tomato sauce and canned tomatoes are essential for Mexican and Italian dishes. Whole wheat pasta is great for a quick dinner. Dried beans and legumes like lentils and chickpeas are inexpensive, versatile protein sources. It's good to always have a backup of peanut butter and jam in case someone needs a snack or a quick, no-fuss meal. I like to stock several kinds of vinegar, including balsamic, red wine, apple cider, rice, and plain old white vinegar. These make many dishes unique, including potato salad, coleslaw, and the perfect chopped salad.

A variety of nuts is also good to have on hand. I like to keep almonds, walnuts, and peanuts available for snacking and baking. Dried fruit, such as raisins, dates, and dried apples, are also great to have for those times when fresh fruit isn't available. Nuts and dried fruit can be whirled together in the food processor to make homemade energy bars (page 105).

Having several different grains in the pantry is important for maintaining a varied diet. Brown rice is a whole grain that can accompany just about anything. Cornmeal helps keep things interesting with polenta or cornbread. Shredded coconut is a key to my homemade granola (page 78), and popcorn kernels assure that a last-minute snack is always possible. I panic when we run out of oats because oatmeal and granola are two of my favorite easy breakfasts. Quinoa is an ancient power grain, providing a complete protein and a unique texture.

Warning

Nearly 90 percent of the corn produced in the United States is genetically modified. Genetically modified organisms (GMOs) have been associated with health problems and environmental damage. Over sixty countries have limitations or bans on GMOs, but they're sold without regulation in the U.S. and Canada. When shopping for products including corn, such as corn meal and popcorn kernels, look for organic or Non-GMO Verified products to avoid possible health risks.

FRUIT BOWL AND VEGGIE DRAWER. One of the best things you can do to stay healthy is to eat lots and lots of produce. The World Health Organization recommends that people eat at least five servings of fruits and vegetables every day. This can be difficult to achieve if we aren't intentional about it. My family goes through a lot of fruit, and I like to keep the fruit bowl stocked with a wide variety of goodies. I often buy fruit that's on sale, which helps me to avoid buying the same fruit over and over.

It can be a harder sell with children, but it's important to eat a wide variety of vegetables, too. Eating seasonally will help you to rotate many different vegetables through your diet. I like to keep onions, garlic, and potatoes on hand at all times. These versatile veggies add flavor and texture to many different dishes. Green vegetables are a step above the rest, and I try to serve green veggies just about every day. Chapter Six is full of delicious recipes that feature vegetables.

Organic produce is a good investment if you can afford it. If you're not sure which fruits and vegetables are best to buy organic, refer to Appendix 3, pg 231. This chart of the "Dirty Dozen and Clean Fifteen" shows which fruits and vegetables have the most pesticides and which ones have the least.

FREEZER STOCKPILE. I typically get a big influx of produce in the summer and fall when things are in season. My freezer allows me to store the summer bounty and enjoy it all through the winter. I generally keep vegetables like corn, chopped onions, pumpkin purée, spinach, and butternut squash in my freezer. Berries and frozen bananas are also great to have in the freezer. As long as I have them on hand, smoothies and banana bread are not far behind. I like to keep a backup supply of chicken broth and bread in the freezer as well. If there's always a backup, I don't have to worry about running out of something just when I need it.

With an organized, well-stocked kitchen, you can save time and money while maintaining sanity as well. Good organization is the first step in taking control of your kitchen. Once everything is in its proper place, you're ready to come up with a well-polished system for planning meals and getting groceries. These will lay the groundwork for Part Two, when we'll get cooking.

Chapter Two

What's on the Menu?

When I was in college, I babysat for a family that lived across the street from the campus. They had the sweetest little three-year-old boy and one-year-old girl. The first time I babysat for them, their mother told me what I was to feed them for dinner that night. She pointed at a piece of paper on the fridge with a handwritten meal schedule for the week. That night, it was spaghetti and meatballs.

Twenty years later, I can still picture that piece of paper. It was only Monday, and they already knew what was for dinner on Friday. I had never seen or thought of a meal plan before. I remember thinking, "Wow, these people are *very* organized." At the time, it seemed a bit extreme.

Benefits of a Meal Plan

Now that I'm a parent running my own kitchen, I realize that it wasn't extreme at all. It was brilliant. Without a plan of attack, it's nearly impossible to stay consistent at serving home-cooked meals. Dinner doesn't magically materialize by itself, and wandering through the grocery store at 5:00 pm looking for inspiration is rarely a good idea. Putting together a weekly meal plan is one of the best habits to develop when you transition to a homemade lifestyle.

MEAL PLANNING SAVES TIME. If you don't have a plan, you'll have to make extra trips to the grocery store to pick up what you need from one day to the next. This takes time away from other things you could be doing. Multiple times each day, you'll have to stop what you're doing to decide about the next meal. You'll find yourself rummaging through the fridge and pantry, asking the nagging question, "What do we have to eat?" It's much more efficient to sit down and decide everything at once.

MEAL PLANNING SAVES MONEY. Extra trips to the store mean extra spending. Impulse purchases are hard to avoid when you go to the store. Also, if you don't have a meal plan in place, you're more likely to buy processed food, take-out, or restaurant meals. These typically cost more than their homemade counterparts. With a meal plan in place, you can control your grocery spending and manage your budget.

MEAL PLANNING YIELDS HEALTHIER MEALS. Homemade food is just about always better for you than processed food or take-out. By making it yourself, you can control the ingredients in your meals. Processed food typically contains high amounts of sodium, sugar, and additives. In fact, many highly-processed foods do more harm than good to your body. They may fill your stomach until the next meal, but they don't provide much in the way of protein, fiber, vitamins, or other nutrients your body needs.

Food Quality Caution

Many Americans have health problems that are caused by eating a highly-processed diet. More than 75 percent of the sodium Americans eat comes from processed or restaurant food, and half of our calories come from processed food. This *Standard American Diet* has been associated with health problems including high blood pressure, heart disease, and obesity.

MEAL PLANNING MAKES LIFE LESS STRESSFUL. On occasion, I don't get around to meal planning. When that happens, I always feel like there's a cloud over my head until I know what's for dinner. Even if I'm looking at a high prep meal one night, I feel relaxed and in control because I know what I need to do. The prospect of a late-afternoon walk through the grocery store looking for inspiration is not pleasant for me. Having a plan in place is the only way to keep this stress out of the picture.

Gathering Meal Planning Resources

It's so easy to get stuck in a rut when it comes to creating a healthy meal plan. The first thing to do is create a master list of all the "go-to" homemade recipes you and your family enjoy. At my house, this list includes things like chili, quiche, whole grain pasta with sauce, and tacos. These are all easy, low-stress dishes that often anchor our meal plans.

You can put together your master list of recipes in a spreadsheet or on a piece of paper. Online meal planning tools often provide an area for this type of list as well. It's a good idea to regularly update this list as you add successful dishes to your repertoire. You will find many of the recipes in this book are designed to become "go-to" recipes that you'll feel comfortable putting on your master list, even if you're still a novice in the kitchen. All the recipes in this book take 30 minutes or less to prepare, so they'll work for you even on a hectic night.

I also suggest trying at least one new recipe each week. You can find inspiration online from your favorite food websites, blogs, or Pinterest. Cookbooks and magazines can give you new ideas, too. I have a folder that's full of recipes ripped out of magazines and photocopied from cookbooks at the library. When I need some fresh ideas, I just flip through these pages.

There are lots of great recipes online, but you should get off the computer on occasion and talk to friends and relatives to find out what meals their families like. When I pick my kids up from school, we often end up on the playground for a while. I chat with other parents there, and sometimes the conversation veers toward food. I love hearing what my friends are making and what their kids are willing to try. It's helpful to talk about the struggles we all have in common when putting dinner on the table.

If you have kids, it's a great idea to have them pick something for the meal plan each week and help prepare it. They'll be more likely to try new foods if they're involved in the planning and preparation process. Kids' cookbooks or old classics like *Joy of Cooking* can provide inspiration as your kids come up with their ideas for the week.

STRUCTURING YOUR MEAL PLAN. For most people, the hardest part of creating a meal plan is making themselves do it. Deciding that meal planning is important and setting aside 15 minutes a week to put the plan together is the essential first step. It may not be fun to sit there and rack your brain about what to serve for dinner, but the relief you'll feel once you have a plan in place is so worth it. I never feel like sitting down to make a meal plan, but I'm so happy when it's done. Here is a template that you can use for your own meal plan.

WEEKLY MEAL PLAN

WEEK OF:_____

	BREAKFAST	LUNCH	DINNER	SNACKS
SUNDAY				
MONDAY				
TUESDAY				
WEDNESDAY				
THURSDAY				
FRIDAY				
SATURDAY				

Writing down your meal plan each week will keep you organized, and your family will appreciate knowing what's coming up on the menu.

SET A SYSTEM. Some people like to plan a month's worth of meals at a time. Others are lucky if they schedule meals 48 hours ahead of time. I like to plan one week at a time because that's what works best for me. I consider what's on sale at the grocery store each week before setting my menu. Also, I get a weekly farm share for half the year, and I don't know what vegetables I'll be receiving until I pick them up. Since I get my farm share on Wednesday and the grocery sale flyers on Thursday, I'm ready to make a plan by Friday.

Those of us who are creatures of habit do well with general guidelines that repeat from one week to the next. For example, you could have Mexican food every Tuesday, pasta every Wednesday, and soup every Friday. There are so many different variations under each of these themes, but it can help guide you as you plug in different ideas.

PLAN MEALS AND SNACKS. To make your meal plan, pick out a variety of foods for each meal of the day. Come up with at least three or four different breakfasts, lunches, dinners, *and* snacks that you'll eat throughout the week. Look at what's on sale and what you have on hand, and try to use up the food that's already sitting in your fridge. This is more practical and affordable than setting a meal plan based solely on what pops into your mind when you sit down to write the plan. For example, if I have a random selection of vegetables that are ready to use, I'll put vegetable soup in the meal plan. But if I don't have many vegetables on hand, this soup wouldn't make much sense.

VARY YOUR FOOD OPTIONS. We all know that we're supposed to eat a "varied diet." This is the hardest part of meal planning, in my opinion, but also the most important one.

Rotating your diet is one of the best things you can do for your health. This means that you shouldn't eat the same things day after day, even "healthy" foods. For example, if you eat oatmeal for breakfast six days a week, your body may develop a sensitivity to oats. By repeating the same small group of foods, people deprive their bodies of nutrients in other foods that they're not eating. Choose different types of grains, produce, and protein sources to cover your meals from one day to the next.

Definition: Rotation Diet

A Rotation Diet is a way of eating that focuses on expanding the variety of food in a person's diet. Foods that are eaten on the first day of the week are avoided until later in the week. This can help prevent food allergies and sensitivities from developing.

If the prospect of planning a week's worth of breakfasts, lunches, dinners, and snacks seems daunting, start by planning just dinner. It's easier to "wing it" with breakfast, lunch, and snacks, but dinner never falls into place by itself. Once you get used to planning your dinner schedule, add in the other meals.

When you plan your dinners, consult your family calendar first. Evenings that are busy with sports or other activities will require quick prep dinners or slow cooker meals. If you want to try a new recipe, save it for a night when you'll be home without interruptions.

RECORD YOUR MEAL PLAN. A chalkboard in the kitchen is a fun way to record your meal plan. It has the added benefit of avoiding the daily "What's for dinner?" question from the kids. A weekly meal planning calendar can also be printed out and you can jot down all your meals for the week. In addition, there are many resources online for meal planning. See page 45 for my blank weekly meal plan template, as well as Appendix 5, pg 235 for some online meal planning services.

I use a calendar on my computer to record my meal plans. One of my favorite things about this method is that if I'm out of ideas for dinner, I can look back to see what we ate in previous months. When my schedule is especially crazy one week, I can simply copy an old meal plan and paste it into the week ahead.

Tip

Your freezer can be your best friend when it comes to feeding your family. These ten dishes are great to keep on hand in your freezer to grab on a busy night. Store them in single-serve portions if you'll want to pull out a serving for one.

- Chili (p. 159)
- Black Bean Soup (p. 161)
- Marinara Sauce (p. 166)
- Baked Pasta Casserole (p. 167)
- Cooked chicken (p. 174)
- Mashed potatoes (p. 137)
- Carrot Soup (p. 148)
- Butternut squash apple soup (p. 149)
- Potato leek soup (p. 151)
- Corn chowder (p. 152)

MAKE ADJUSTMENTS ALONG THE WAY. I make a weekly meal plan, but it's never perfect. Schedule changes can jump in the way. A late-afternoon work meeting goes long and you're not home in time to start cooking what you had intended. A Little League game that was supposed to be on Tuesday gets rained out, and it's rescheduled for Wednesday. You were supposed to be sitting around the table with your family and a steaming bowl of chili on Wednesday, but now you find yourself on the baseball sidelines at dinnertime instead.

Don't let these snafus shake your resolve. Don't think the only thing you can do is admit defeat and order pizza. Life happens, and you and your meal plan can learn to roll with it. My meal plan is a great guide, but it tends to be a fluid document.

If you have enough lead time, you can swap Tuesday's dinner plan for Wednesday in the example above. If not, it's helpful to have a few healthy "Plan B" meals that can be ready on short notice. I always try to freeze extra portions of a few different meals for times like these. Things like calzones and burritos can be made ahead and frozen. They're perfect to take along to sporting events or other evening dinnertime interrupters.

Sample Meal Plans

Learning how to put your favorite meals together into a schedule is a vital kitchen skill that every adult should master. When you're just getting started, though, it's nice to see what other people's meal plans look like. Part Two of this book includes lots of easy, healthy recipes, and I've put together two weekly meal plans using these recipes. It's best to eat produce that's in season, so you can substitute any fruits or vegetables that are available.

WEEKLY MEAL PLAN

WEEK OF:_____

*Page number for the Recipe -

	BREAKFAST	LUNCH	DINNER	SNACKS
SUNDAY	Pancakes with bananas and pure maple syrup *220	Corn Chowder *152	Homemade pizza *225	Chocolate energy bar, melon *105
MONDAY	Oatmeal with banana *74	Vegetarian chili with cornbread *159	Baked pasta casserole, broccoli salad *167	Popcorn, cheese and crackers *113
TUESDAY	Scrambled eggs, sautéed kale, melon *82	Pesto and sundried tomato sandwich on whole grain bread *146	Sloppy Joes over baked potatoes, green salad *178	Apple, hummus and carrot sticks *112
WEDNESDAY	Yogurt with berries and walnuts *95	Corn Chowder *152	Maple Salmon, baked potato, kale chips *179	Chocolate energy bar, orange *105
THURSDAY	Apple Pie Overnight Oats *76	Vegetarian chili with cornbread *159/181	Baked pasta casserole, broccoli salad *167	Carrot muffin, popcorn *119/113
FRIDAY	Fried eggs, whole grain toast, melon *85	Asian rice noodle bowl *185	Sloppy Joes over baked potatoes, green salad *178/136	Apple, hummus and red pepper strips *112
SATURDAY	Granola *78	Butternut Squash Apple Soup *149	Taco Night *160	Cucumbers with ranch dip, almonds *216

(Download full-sized versions at http://ConqueringYourKitchen.com)

BREAKING DOWN THE MEAL PLAN. This meal plan includes a variety of different fruits, vegetables, grains, and protein sources. Some people live by the adage, "An apple a day keeps the doctor away." I don't really go for this idea. An apple every two or three days is great. But if you eat an apple every day, think of all the other fruits you're not eating. Berries, melons, pineapples, and pears all have unique nutrients that your body wants. Don't get me wrong – I adore apples. They're one of my favorite quick, healthy snacks, and I love to bake them into just about anything. But if we eat the same few fruits day after day for weeks on end, our bodies won't get everything they need. Several foods are repeated a few times throughout the week in this meal plan, but there's nothing that we're eating every day.

For breakfast, I included two days of oatmeal and two days of eggs. Granola is on the menu for one morning. Since it's made mostly from oats, I only have it for one day because I don't want to have oats more than three times in the week. Remember, variety is key. Yogurt and pancakes round out this week's breakfast menu.

I like to schedule filling meals for lunchtime. It can be a long stretch between lunch and dinner, so if I don't fuel up at lunchtime, I'll be reaching for snacks throughout the afternoon. It's all too easy to grab convenient, nutrient-deficient packaged foods in the afternoon. In this meal plan, I have hearty soups and chili for lunch most days. I make big batches of soup, and I freeze them in single-serve portions so they're ready to go for lunches. The meal plan also includes a sandwich and an Asian noodle bowl for lunches on the other days.

For the dinner menu, I included a big baked pasta casserole that covers two nights. This dish keeps well in the fridge, so I use it for Monday and Thursday. Homemade pizza and Taco Night are popular meals where everyone can assemble their own ingredients according to their tastes. Sloppy Joes are easy to make, and they keep well for leftovers. My kids don't love fish, but I like to include it in our dinner menu a couple times a month. It's a good source of Omega-3 fatty acids, which are essential for brain health. With a splash of maple syrup or another tasty topping, everyone is usually willing to eat it.

I include fruits and vegetables at snack time almost every day. It's hard to reach your daily produce quota of "five a day" without being intentional about it. This is part of why meal planning is so helpful. Popcorn is one of the easiest whole grain snacks to make, so it shows up regularly on our snack menu. A handful of nuts is an even easier snack, and it gives a good burst of protein to help maintain your energy. Hummus, homemade snack bars, and muffins are also included in this meal plan. I always keep some homemade muffins in the freezer so I can defrost them for a healthy, tasty snack.

WEEKLY MEAL PLAN

WEEK OF:_____

*Page number for the Recipe -

	BREAKFAST	LUNCH	DINNER	SNACKS
SUNDAY	Waffles with berries and pure maple syrup *91	Asian chicken salad *186	Pasta with marinara sauce, green salad *166	Lemon Blueberry muffin, almonds *118
MONDAY	Fruit Smoothie, toast with peanut butter *98	Mediterranean quinoa salad *187	Lemon Broccoli Pasta *170	Roasted chickpeas, apple *110
TUESDAY	Egg in a Hole, melon *86	Potato Leek Soup, green salad *151	Vegetable Calzones *226	Cranberry bread, popcorn *122
WEDNESDAY	Oatmeal with diced apples and cinnamon # 74	Lemon Broccoli Pasta * 170	Whole Chicken in the Slow Cooker, asparagus, roasted potatoes *174/*135	Granola Bar, mango * 107
THURSDAY	Breakfast Casserole *87	Mediterranean quinoa salad *187	Tuna cornbread casserole *181	Roasted chickpeas, orange *110
FRIDAY	Granola with yogurt and berries * 78	Carrot soup, grilled cheese *148	Chicken quesadillas with corn tortillas, green salad	Banana bread, melon *120
SATURDAY	Breakfast Casserole *87	Potato Leek Soup, coleslaw *151	Lentil Sweet Potato Casserole *163	Granola Bar, carrot sticks *107

(Download full-sized versions at http://ConqueringYourKitchen.com)

BREAKING DOWN THE MEAL PLAN. In the Week Two meal plan, breakfast has a variety of fun combinations. Eggs are featured on three of the days, and this will keep everyone full well into the morning. Smoothies, oatmeal, and granola are quick breakfasts for the other weekdays. On Sunday, it's time for a nice sit-down waffle breakfast. I think it's a great idea to take the time for a slow family breakfast at least once a week, and the weekend is often the best time for this.

Mediterranean quinoa salad is featured twice on this week's lunch menu. The Lemon Broccoli Pasta from Monday's dinner keeps well in the fridge, so it makes a great leftover lunch on Wednesday. Soups that can be made ahead and frozen cover the other lunch slots, in addition to an Asian chicken salad on Sunday.

On this week's dinner menu, we see a whole chicken on Wednesday served with potatoes and asparagus. Then it makes another appearance on Friday in the form of chicken quesadillas. If you have enough chicken, you can make extra quesadillas to freeze for lunches on a future meal plan. Calzones are a great addition to the menu for a night when you're running around to sports practices or other extracurricular dinnertime interruptions. Pasta, tuna cornbread casserole, and lentil casserole are easy, healthy dinners that fill out the other evenings.

For snack time, roasted chickpeas are featured as a high-protein snack item that can be surprisingly addictive. Homemade granola bars are another higher-protein treat that can help sustain you from one meal to the next. As with the Week One meal plan, I also include fruit and vegetables for snack most days. Homemade breads, muffins, and popcorn round out this week's snack menu.

I know the meal planning process may seem overwhelming at first, but it's so worth it. Having a meal plan in place makes life less stressful and it makes mealtime healthier. Meal planning will help you to save money and time, too. You have to intentionally make time for meal planning if you want to truly master your kitchen.

When I babysat that family back in college, I thought they were a bit neurotic when I saw their meal plan on the fridge. Now, I know that they were right on the money.

Chapter Three
Mastering the Grocery Puzzle

One of the best ways to minimize stress when it comes to feeding a family is having a well-stocked kitchen full of healthy food options. There's security in knowing that you can put together a baked pasta casserole on a moment's notice if unexpected guests stop over at dinnertime. An unplanned playdate is a breeze if you have popcorn kernels in the cabinet.

Stocking up on the right ingredients takes time, patience, and planning, but it's well worth it in the end. Grocery shopping is a part of every household, and having a good system is essential. With the right plan of attack, buying food doesn't have to be a dreaded chore. Setting a food budget, deciding where to shop, and organizing your shopping with a list are the keys to mastering the grocery puzzle.

Grocery store options can feel overwhelming. Learn to simplify this process!

Setting a Food Budget

Food spending is an area of a family's budget that has a lot of wiggle room. Unlike the electric bill or taxes, you have a good bit of control over how much money you spend on food purchases. Many American families spend between 15 and 20 percent of their monthly income on food. This includes groceries as well as restaurant meals. Determining your family's food budget is the important first step of the grocery shopping puzzle.

EVERY FAMILY'S FOOD BUDGET IS UNIQUE. One family makes it a priority to buy organic produce and grass-fed meat, while another focuses on gluten-free ingredients due to a food allergy. Still another family likes to eat out a few times a week to take a break from the kitchen. Before setting a budget, evaluate your family's needs and decide what types of food you're willing to spend more to get.

Priority-Setting Tip

To help determine your family's food priorities, consult some of the books and movies that have come out addressing food justice issues. Two helpful films are *Food Inc.* and *Fed Up*. Michael Pollan's book, *In Defense of Food*, is another great resource. See Appendix 5 for more recommended resources.

RESTAURANT BUDGET. Prepared foods and restaurant meals tend to be a lot more expensive than home-cooked food. Restaurants typically charge three times the amount they pay for the ingredients in the meals they serve, so you can save a lot of money by making those meals at home. It's nice to eat out once in a while, but it's a good idea to limit dining at restaurants for both budget and health reasons. By preparing most of your food yourself, you can control what ingredients you're eating.

I recommend that you determine a monthly budget for dining out, and then do your best to stick to it. You'll make exceptions here and there for a special occasion or unexpected invitation to meet friends for dinner, but at least you'll have a baseline. Some families like to include eating out in the "entertainment" section of their budgets. It really doesn't matter where you put it in your budget. The important thing is to be aware of how much you're spending on dining out and to spend your money intentionally.

GROCERY BUDGET. If you don't pay attention to how much money you spend on groceries, the bills can become astronomical. You can easily drop $200 or more on a cart full of groceries at many different stores. It's important to determine how much you want to spend each month on groceries.

A simple way to set your budget initially is to look at your current food spending over a three-month period. I use my credit card for most food purchases, so this is an easy way for me to track how much I'm spending. If you aren't disciplined enough to pay off your credit card bill every month, you can track your spending by paying with cash and saving receipts. Make a spreadsheet to track the total amount you spend each month.

Take a look at the average amount of money you've spent on groceries each month during the three month period. There will be some variation from one month to the next, but focus on the average. This number is your starting point.

The ideal grocery budget is both challenging and realistic at the same time. To bring down your food spending, set an initial monthly budget at $25 less than the average you came up with from the three-month period. For a month or two, keep track of spending and see if you can meet this lower number. If it's going pretty easily for you, cut another $25 and see how that works. Once you get to the point where it's almost a struggle to meet your grocery budget but you can do it without too much angst, you've found the right number.

Warning

Sale prices can be difficult to resist, but proceed with caution. Don't buy junk just because you can get a good deal on it. It's tempting to buy something because it's a good price, even though you don't need it. If you're trying to stick to a budget and maintain a healthy homemade diet, there will be many great bargains out there that you'll want to avoid. Stay focused on the fact that you want to save money on *high-quality food*, and this will help guide you through the many shopping decisions that you face.

Over the years, I've learned how to trim my grocery bill quite a bit. Our current grocery budget is $550, and it feeds four of us for a month. I used to spend more than this on food when it was just my husband and I eating a more processed diet before our kids were born. Some months it's a struggle to stick to the food budget, but I just think about the money we're saving that will pay for that next vacation. I love to travel with my family, and this keeps me motivated.

Shopping for Food from Various Sources

Once you have a budget in hand, the next step is to assess the shopping options in your area. I live in a densely populated metropolitan area, so there are dozens of grocery stores within ten miles of my house. There are farmers' markets in every town and several warehouse stores at my disposal. In more rural areas, the options are much more limited. In some ways, this scenario is easier. If there's only one market around, you don't have to think too much about where to shop.

If you live in an area with lots of shopping options, it's a good idea to get a sense of all the stores. Compare prices on the items you regularly buy at the different stores. I actually keep a price chart where I list the best prices for all the food items I stock regularly. If you're not a type-A like me, you can do a more informal price comparison. Hopefully this comparison will clarify which store or stores you'll want to visit most often.

Getting Fresh Produce

A healthy diet includes fruits or vegetables at just about every meal and snack. Many of us can get overwhelmed by the produce options in the grocery store, and it's hard to know what to buy. For years, I only bought broccoli, carrots, potatoes, bananas, apples, and pears. I wasn't sure what to do with the rest of it, so I stuck to the safe fruits and veggies that were most familiar to me. Because produce is the most important and often most challenging part of a healthy lifestyle, let's look at some of the places to find it.

CSA/FARM SHARE. Several years ago, my produce shopping changed dramatically. I had wanted to join a CSA for years, but I was nervous to try it. Through Community Supported Agriculture, consumers pay a farmer one lump sum at the beginning of the growing season and they get a share of the farm's produce each week. I wasn't sure if my family would be adventurous enough to try all the new produce we'd be getting. I also didn't know how I'd have the time to prepare all these new foods. As it turned out, I had nothing to worry about. I fell in love immediately, and my family has been enjoying delicious, organic, local produce ever since.

Tip for Storing Greens

Storing greens properly will dramatically extend their life. When you come home with lettuce, kale, basil, or other greens and herbs, wash their full leaves (not chopped) in the bowl of a salad spinner. Wash until the grit is gone, and dry them completely. Store each set of greens in its own airtight container with a paper towel on the bottom and the top of the pile of greens. With this method, lettuce should last for a week and herbs can last up to two weeks.

A farm share can be much more affordable than the grocery store for fresh, local produce. The food tastes better because you get it right after it's harvested, and there's a bounty in the summer that can be preserved for the winter. My favorite part of belonging to a CSA is that it imposes variety and helps dictate meal planning. I never bought squash, eggplant, or kale before, but now my family eats them. Once these "different" veggies make their way from the farm to my produce drawer, I find a way to enjoy them. To locate a farm share in your area, visit Localharvest.org.

Farmers' markets carry all sorts of local produce and locally made products.

FARMERS' MARKET. Another great place to get local produce is a farmers' market. These seem to be cropping up everywhere these days. Over the past 20 years, there's been a steady growth of farmers' markets in the U.S., with over 8,000 markets nationwide in 2014. Although the prices here are more expensive than in a farm share, you have greater control over what food you'll be getting. If the prices make you hesitant about stocking your kitchen with farmers' market food, start small.

Bring $10 to the market and see how much you can bring home. If your children are with you at the market, give them a couple dollars and tell them they can pick out any unprocessed food they want. This is a great way to get them to try something new. To find a farmers' market near you, visit Eatlocalgrown.com.

GROCERY STORES. Each week, I end up purchasing some of my produce at the grocery store. Living in a cold climate like Massachusetts, our growing season is limited to the warmer months. We really like bananas and avocados, and there's nowhere to get them around here other than at the grocery store. I read the sales flyers weekly to see what produce items are on sale, and that helps dictate my purchases. I also regularly visit the "reduced produce" cart, where I can often get slightly bruised goodies for apple crisp or zucchini bread. If you can't afford to buy everything organic, keep in mind that some conventionally grown produce contains more pesticide residue than others. See the "Dirty Dozen/Clean 15" chart in Appendix 3 for details.

GROW YOUR OWN. The most affordable place to get great produce is your own backyard. We have very little sun in our modest suburban yard, but I still manage to grow basil, chives, raspberries, and a few other goodies every summer. Even if you live in a small apartment in the city, you can grow herbs and tomatoes in pots on the balcony. There's nothing like the satisfaction of plucking something off a vine or a stalk in your own yard and popping it into your mouth. For more ideas about growing your own food see *Backyard Farming on an Acre (More or Less)* at http://BackyardFarmingGuide.com.

Shopping for Other Groceries

I shop for most of my non-produce food at conventional grocery stores, including Stop & Shop, Trader Joe's, and Whole Foods Market. When shopping for groceries at conventional stores, it's best to shop the perimeter of the store. That's where most of the whole foods are located. Lots of highly-processed food is lurking in the aisles, so you don't want to spend much time there. I do make strategic strikes for things like dried beans, rice, and oatmeal. I read labels and look for single-ingredient items. Instead of buying oatmeal packets that have a long list of flavorings and chemicals, I buy single-ingredient rolled oats and add flavor at home.

Warehouse stores are another great option, especially if you're feeding a family. At Costco, I can get some organic items like tomato sauce for less than the price of their conventional counterparts at the regular grocery store. By stocking up on items like oats and applesauce, I don't have to run out to the store as often. This helps to avoid those annoying impulse purchases. Items tend to cost less when you buy them in large quantities, but be sure not to stock up on something that your family won't be able to finish before the expiration date.

With my busy family life and work commitments, I'm not able to avoid processed food altogether. As a rule of thumb, when I'm buying packaged foods I read the ingredient lists, looking for items with about five or fewer ingredients. All the ingredients should be things I can pronounce and things I might cook with at home. If I'm shopping for crackers, for example, I'll look for a type that has nothing more than flour, oil, and salt. There's no need to buy the flavored versions that contain long, hard-to-pronounce ingredient lists.

Caution

If you're buying packaged food, look for short ingredient lists with words that you can pronounce. If there's something on the list that you couldn't cook with at home, you want to avoid buying that item. Keep looking on the shelves because there's usually a better option or you can find a recipe to make it at home.

If you don't have great grocery stores in your area, you can get a lot of high-quality grocery items online. Look at websites like Amazon.com and Vitacost.com to search for items you can't easily get near you. Things like coconut oil and gluten-free flour can often be found for less online, and you don't even have to leave your house to buy them.

Organizing Your Shopping with a List

I'm a little neurotic about grocery lists. If I don't stick to a very organized system, I can easily spend an extra hundred dollars a month on groceries. I end up going to the store four or five times a week because I'm not on top of what we need in the house. One of the most important shopping skills to master is making a list and sticking to it at the store.

Avoid Unnecessary Shopping Trips

Don't leave the store without knowing you have everything you need. Keep a master list of items that you regularly purchase. Review this list before you leave for the store, and you won't have to keep making extra shopping trips every few days for "just a few things." Those extra trips are budget-killers every time.

Back in my early twenties, I worked on the staff of the Jesuit Volunteer Corps, a Catholic volunteer program. This was a time in my life when I knew next to nothing about shopping or cooking. We had several retreat weekends throughout the year where we had to feed 70 volunteers. I didn't have to do the cooking, but I was part of the meal planning and shopping team. I remember the sense of amazement that hit me the first time I saw the "Master Shopping List."

This master list was built on the wisdom of retreat planners who had gone before me. It included everything you could possibly need to feed 70 people several different types of meals. One priest who attended the retreats liked to make pancakes for the participants on Sunday mornings, so the master list told us exactly what we'd need for those pancakes. Taco Night was a popular menu selection that worked well for both vegetarians and omnivores. All the fixings for Taco Night were right there on that master list as well. Plates, forks, knives, napkins, and lemonade mix – it was all there on the list. With proper planning, you couldn't possibly forget something at the store.

Fast forward two decades. I'm only feeding a family of four now, but I've made a master list for our groceries as well. It's an ever-growing spreadsheet that includes all the basics we regularly eat. I've assessed which of my grocery stores has the best price for each item, and that information is on the list too.

Warning: Shopping Hungry

Don't go shopping for groceries when you're hungry. It's almost guaranteed that you'll make extra purchases because everything looks *so* good when your stomach is growling. My weakness at those moments is potato chips. Have a healthy snack before you go to the store so you can stay disciplined and stick to your list.

We have a notepad on our refrigerator where everyone in the family can write down the grocery items we need. Instead of writing things on your grocery list when you run out of them, write them on the list when you *open* the last package. When it's time for a trip to the store, I look at that refrigerator list along with my meal plan and my master list.

If I'm going to Trader Joe's, I can sort my master list for Trader Joe's. I then go through the cabinets and fridge to see where we're running low. I try to stock up on a month's worth of Trader Joe's groceries so I don't end up overspending on impulse purchases.

Their seasonal processed goodies are impossibly tempting, so I know I need to limit my time in that store.

Shopping List in Action: Two Week Meal Plan

In chapter two, there are two examples of weekly meal plans. These plans won't get past the "idea" phase unless you actually get out to the store and buy what you need to make the meals. Below you'll find a comprehensive shopping list that will allow you to make all these recipes. But unless you're starting out with completely empty cabinets, you probably won't need to buy everything on this list. For example, if you already have oats on hand, you're covered for several of the breakfast meals. Also, if you're making things like homemade sandwich bread, ricotta (p. 213), or chicken broth (p.175), you won't need to buy them either.

It's helpful to organize your shopping list in the order that you find the items in your grocery store. The list below presumes that you'll start in the produce section and move around the periphery of the store. The last part of the list includes items that are found in the aisles. You don't want to linger in the aisles or you're bound to come home with highly processed snacks that aren't on your list. Consult the recipes in the meal plans for quantities of each item according to how many family members you'll be serving.

SHOPPING LIST
FOR MEAL PLANS

PRODUCE:
- [ ] apples, fresh
- [ ] apples, dried
- [ ] asparagus
- [ ] bananas
- [ ] basil
- [ ] berries
- [ ] broccoli
- [ ] butternut squash
- [ ] cranberries
- [ ] cucumber
- [ ] garlic
- [ ] ginger
- [ ] green beans
- [ ] kale
- [ ] leeks
- [ ] lemon
- [ ] lime
- [ ] lettuce
- [ ] mandarin oranges
- [ ] mangoes
- [ ] Medjool dates
- [ ] melon
- [ ] onion, white
- [ ] onion, red
- [ ] oranges
- [ ] peas
- [ ] potatoes, red skin
- [ ] potatoes, russet
- [ ] raisins
- [ ] scallions
- [ ] sweet pepper (1 rd, 2 grn)
- [ ] sweet potatoes

MEAT:
- [ ] bacon
- [ ] ground beef or turkey
- [ ] salmon
- [ ] whole chicken

DAIRY:
- [ ] butter
- [ ] cheddar cheese
- [ ] eggs
- [ ] milk
- [ ] mozzarella cheese
- [ ] parmesan cheese
- [ ] ricotta
- [ ] yogurt

BAKERY:
- [ ] corn tortillas
- [ ] whole grain bread

BAKING AISLE:
- [ ] whole wheat flour
- [ ] cornmeal
- [ ] cocoa powder
- [ ] coconut, shredded unsweetened
- [ ] active dry yeast
- [ ] baking powder
- [ ] baking soda
- [ ] cinnamon
- [ ] smoked paprika
- [ ] curry powder
- [ ] onion powder
- [ ] chili powder
- [ ] cumin
- [ ] oregano
- [ ] mustard powder
- [ ] salt
- [ ] sugar
- [ ] vanilla extract

OTHER AISLES:
- [ ] peanut butter
- [ ] walnuts
- [ ] almonds
- [ ] cashews
- [ ] sesame seeds
- [ ] brown rice cereal
- [ ] oats
- [ ] dried black beans
- [ ] dried pinto beans
- [ ] dried kidney beans
- [ ] dried chickpeas
- [ ] dried lentils
- [ ] white vinegar
- [ ] red wine vinegar
- [ ] rice vinegar
- [ ] olive oil
- [ ] coconut oil
- [ ] sesame oil
- [ ] soy sauce
- [ ] tahini (optional)
- [ ] chicken or vegetable broth
- [ ] canned whole tomatoes
- [ ] canned crushed tomatoes
- [ ] tomato sauce
- [ ] sundried tomatoes
- [ ] mayonnaise
- [ ] honey
- [ ] maple syrup
- [ ] applesauce
- [ ] brown rice noodles
- [ ] whole wheat pasta
- [ ] brown rice crisp cereal
- [ ] popcorn kernels
- [ ] whole grain crackers
- [ ] quinoa
- [ ] Kalamata olives
- [ ] tuna

Full-sized versions available at http//ConqueringYourKitchen.com

It's best to eat produce seasonally, so I recommend substituting fruits and vegetables that are readily available in your market for the ones listed in the meal plan once you get more comfortable making meal plans on your own. Just remember that variety is key. You probably have several of the baking supplies and "other aisles" items in your pantry already, so this will help to cut back the list.

Sticking to your shopping list is essential if you want to keep a reasonable grocery budget. Grocery stores are *designed* to get you to buy things you weren't planning to buy. Food companies pay big money to have their items placed on end caps and at eye level in the aisles. Don't let marketers determine what you buy. If you make a list ahead of time and stay true to it, that next vacation can stay within reach.

With all this nutritious food on hand, you're ready to move to Part Two. Grab your wooden spoon, because it's time to get cooking.

Part Two
Get Cooking

In Part Two, we look at many aspects of the cooking process. This part is full of information and tips to help you master the art of preparing healthy, affordable homemade food. I will guide you through easy recipes and cooking techniques that will make you look like a pro in the kitchen.

CHAPTER FOUR
THE BREAKFAST SCRAMBLE

We've all heard that breakfast is the most important meal of the day. A proper breakfast sets us up with the energy we need to face the tasks ahead. Some people skip breakfast, but I couldn't possibly function without breakfast. I wake up famished in the morning. Breakfast is part of the "waking up" process for me, and it's my favorite meal. I love waffles and eggs and oatmeal and breakfast burritos. There's a lot of tempting food on a breakfast menu.

Because of its timing, breakfast can be the trickiest meal to get on the table. With work or school looming in the morning, it's natural to look for something quick and easy at breakfast time. Many people stick with boxed cereal, packaged granola bars, or a piece of toast to go with their cup of coffee in the morning. This is fine on occasion, but it doesn't provide the best breakfast to keep you full and energized until it's time for lunch.

There are two keys to ensuring you'll have a variety of hearty breakfasts ready on busy weekday mornings. First, make a weekly meal plan ahead of time so you don't have to deal with decisions in the groggy haze of morning. With a plan in place, you can make sure you have all the ingredients needed for breakfast each day. Second, prepare what you can the night before so you don't have too much prep in the morning. If you're having oatmeal, you can soak it in water overnight so it's ready for the stovetop when you wake up. For pancakes, make the batter in the evening so all you need to do in the morning is fire up the griddle. With just a little planning and prep work ahead of time, your family's daily breakfast can be nourishing and satisfying.

In this chapter, you'll find a wide range of easy recipes to serve for breakfast. From a simple bowl of oatmeal to a French toast casserole for the weekend, these recipes will help you to provide variety and keep things interesting. You won't be tempted to settle for a bowl of cereal when you have all these simple, delicious recipes at your disposal.

All About Oats

Oats are a wonderful whole grain to include at breakfast. High in fiber and several essential nutrients, a serving of oatmeal includes 5 grams of protein. Adding some diced nuts to your morning oatmeal is a good way to increase the protein and keep you feeling full for a longer period. Berries or bananas are a great accompaniment to round out the meal.

You can buy single-ingredient oats in several forms. They all start out as oat groats, which are hulled, toasted oat grains. The least-processed type of oats you'll find at the store is the steel-cut variety, followed by old fashioned rolled oats and then quick oats. All three of these varieties are nutritious whole grains.

- **Steel Cut Oats:** Oat groats are chopped into little pellets; they require the longest cooking time.
- **Old-Fashioned (Rolled) Oats:** Oat groats are steamed and rolled into flakes.
- **Quick-Cooking Oats:** Old fashioned oats are rolled thinner and chopped more finely to create a faster cook time.

You Can Do Better Than Instant

Instant oatmeal packets aren't a healthy option for breakfast. Full of sugar and other unnecessary additives, they have a much less nourishing profile than the single-ingredient oat options listed above. Leave the instant oatmeal packets on the shelf at the grocery store and flavor your own oatmeal at home.

STOVETOP OATS. Oats are simple to cook on the stove. To make things easier in the morning, I like to soak the oats in a pot of water overnight. When I think of it, I include a tablespoon of lemon juice or whey in the soaking water to help make the oats easier to digest. This form of soaking helps to break down the phytic acid in the oats, which can be difficult to digest and can block the absorption of important minerals.

In the morning, put the pot of oats on the stove and bring it to a near-boil over medium-high heat using the water from the overnight soak. Stay close to the stove during this part, because if you walk away to check your email, you'll likely come back to an overflowing mess. As soon as the bubbles start, turn the heat down to low and simmer with the cover on until the oats are mushy and the liquid is absorbed. For steel-cut oats, this takes 30 minutes. Old-fashioned rolled oats take about 5 minutes to cook, and quick oats are done in 1 minute.

OATMEAL
PREPARATION CHART

STEEL CUT OATS:

Number of servings: 4

Serving size: ¾ cup cooked oatmeal

Amount of water or milk: 4 cups

Amount of oats: 1 cup

Cooking Time: 30 minutes

OLD-FASHIONED ROLLED OATS:

Number of servings: 4

Serving size: ¾ cup cooked oatmeal

Amount of water or milk: 3¼ cups

Amount of oats: 2 cups

Cooking Time: 5 minutes

QUICK OATS:

Number of servings: 4

Serving size: ¾ cup cooked oatmeal

Amount of water or milk: 3½ cups

Amount of oats: 2 cups

Cooking time: 1 minute

APPLE PIE OVERNIGHT OATS. Old-fashioned rolled oats and quick oats don't actually need to be cooked. Some people prefer them that way, but overnight refrigerator oats are an option that tastes a lot like the cooked version. They can be flavored in so many different ways, and they're so convenient. This dish is ready to eat when you wake up in the morning. If you don't have dried apples, you can substitute fresh apples in this recipe.

Yield: 4 servings *Prep Time: 10 minutes*
Serving Size: 1¼ cup

Ingredients:
2½ cups rolled oats
3 cups milk
2 tbsp. plain yogurt
4 Medjool dates, pits
   removed

1½ cups dried apple,
chopped
½ tsp. cinnamon
¼ tsp. ginger

Directions:
1. In a large bowl, stir together the oats, milk, and yogurt.
2. Place the dates and apples in a food processor and finely chop them. Make sure you've removed the pits from the dates or your food processor blade will sound like a helicopter.
3. Stir the dates and apples into the oats and add the cinnamon and ginger.
4. Divide the mixture evenly into four pint-sized mason jars. Cover and refrigerate overnight.
5. In the morning, you can serve this cold. Alternately, warm it up on the stovetop in a small saucepan over medium-low heat. These will keep for several days in the refrigerator.

BLUEBERRY BANANA BAKED OATMEAL. This baked oatmeal is another recipe that you can prepare the night before, and then pop it in the oven when you wake up. The house will smell amazing while this is baking. If you have kids who are sluggish to get out of bed, this aroma just may do the trick.

Yield: 4 servings   *Prep Time: 10 minutes*
Serving Size: 4 x 4 inch piece   *Cook Time: 30 minutes*

Ingredients:

1 ripe banana, mashed   2½ cups rolled oats
1 egg   1 tsp. cinnamon
1½ cups milk   ½ tsp. salt
⅓ cup maple syrup   1 cup blueberries
1 tsp. vanilla extract

Directions:
1. Preheat the oven to 375 degrees and grease an 8 by 8 inch baking dish with butter or coconut oil.
2. Mash the banana in a large bowl. Add the egg, milk, maple syrup, and vanilla extract.
3. In a separate bowl, stir together the oats, cinnamon, and salt.
4. Add the dry ingredients to the wet ingredients and stir until combined.
5. Stir in the blueberries.
6. Bake for 30 minutes, or until the oatmeal is set (no longer watery in the middle). Cool slightly, then cut into four pieces and serve.

The leftovers can be stored in an airtight container in the refrigerator for several days.

Granola is a healthy, delicious make-ahead breakfast that can be made with many different flavor combinations, including this chocolate version.

MAPLE GRANOLA. Homemade granola is one of life's simple pleasures. There are so many ways you can flavor granola, so it never gets boring. Full of whole grains, protein, and dried fruit, homemade granola is a healthier alternative to the boxed cereals we often depend on for a quick, easy breakfast.

Store-bought granola typically contains way too much added sugar, so make this "just sweet enough" granola instead. Play with the proportions to suit your tastes, and experiment with some of the variations listed below the recipe. Granola makes a fantastic breakfast, snack, or even dessert.

Yield: 12 servings
Serving size: ¾ cup

Prep Time: 10 minutes
Cook Time: 60 minutes

Ingredients:

3 cups rolled oats
1½ cups brown rice cereal
1 cup unsweetened dried coconut
2 cups chopped nuts and/or seeds (almonds, cashews, walnuts, sunflower seeds, pumpkin seeds, etc.)

½ tsp. cinnamon
½ cup melted coconut oil
⅓ cup maple syrup
1 tsp. vanilla extract
1 cup dried fruit (raisins, apricots, dried cranberries, etc.)

Directions:

1. Preheat the oven to 275 degrees.
2. Mix the oats, rice cereal, coconut, nuts, and cinnamon in a large bowl.
3. In a small bowl, stir together the coconut oil, maple syrup, and vanilla extract.
4. Pour the liquid over the dry ingredients and stir to coat evenly.
5. Place the mixture in a 9 by 13 inch baking dish and press down the granola to make one even layer.
6. Bake for about an hour, or until it begins to turn light brown and bind together.
7. Place the pan on a wire rack to cool, and let it cool completely before removing the granola.

8. Use a spatula or large spoon to break up the granola. Stir in the dried fruit and store the granola in an airtight container.

Variations:

For peanut butter granola, reduce the nuts to 1 cup and add 2 tablespoons of single-ingredient peanut butter to the wet ingredients.

For chocolate granola, omit the cinnamon and reduce the nuts to 1 cup. Add ¼ cup of cocoa powder to the dry oat mixture.

For pumpkin granola, add ¼ teaspoon of ground ginger to the dry ingredients and ¼ cup of pumpkin purée to the wet ingredients. Dried cranberries are a great complement here.

For your own granola, experiment with different seasonings, extracts, grains, nuts, and dried fruit to come up with your favorite.

Measuring Sticky Ingredients

Maple syrup and honey can be tricky ingredients to transfer from a measuring cup into a mixing bowl. When you pour them, they stick to the sides of the measuring cup and take their sweet time getting into the bowl. Whenever you have a recipe with these ingredients plus oil or butter, measure the oil or butter first. Then measure the maple syrup or honey. The oil will leave behind a slippery residue in the cup, and this will help the sticky sweeteners to slide right out of the measuring cup and into the mixing bowl.

Eggs for Everyone

Eggs are a classic breakfast staple. Packed with protein, vitamins, minerals, and antioxidants, eggs can provide a burst of nutrition at breakfast time. Because they're more filling than some other breakfast options, eggs can help curb cravings later in the day. Eggs are very versatile, and you can serve them next to fruit or vegetables and a piece of toast for a well-rounded meal.

As we discussed in Chapter 1, there's a dizzying array of options when it comes to purchasing eggs at the grocery store. Packages that contain terms like "natural," "hormone-free," and "antibiotic-free" can be deceiving. All eggs currently sold in the U.S. fit into these categories, so these terms don't actually indicate higher quality. Cage-free eggs come from chickens that aren't in cages, but they don't always have access to the outdoors.

Organic, free-range eggs tend to be the best choice at the grocery store if you can afford them. These eggs come from chickens who have unlimited access to fresh food, water, and the outdoors. Their feed is certified organic. Of course, if you can get your hands on eggs from backyard chickens or a local farmer, these can be an even better option. They're fresher than packaged eggs that need time to travel to the grocery store, and you can see their living conditions up close.

Eggs are a versatile food that can be prepared so many different ways. Scrambling, boiling, and frying eggs are some of the most common ways to cook them. Baking them in the form of a quiche or casserole can be even easier. By mastering these basic techniques, you can vary your breakfast menu and nobody will get tired of the same old "over easy" breakfast.

SCRAMBLED EGGS. Scrambled eggs are a simple dish to make when you're cooking for a crowd. Since there's no need to take individual orders, you can cook everyone's eggs at one time. As a rule of thumb, use two eggs for every person you'll be feeding, or cut the number down to one egg for children with smaller appetites. Once you've mastered the basic technique, try some of the variations below the recipe for a unique breakfast scramble.

Yield: 4 servings   *Prep Time: 5 minutes*
Serving Size: 2 eggs   *Cook Time: 5 minutes*

Ingredients:
8 eggs
1 tbsp. butter
2 tbsp. milk or cream (or
more, to taste)
¼ tsp. salt

Directions:
1. Crack the eggs into a large bowl. Use a fork to whip the egg mixture until it has a uniform yellow color. Add the milk and whip it into the eggs with the fork.
2. Place a large, heavy-bottomed skillet on the stove over medium heat. Melt enough butter to coat the skillet.
3. Pour the egg mixture into the skillet and cook over medium heat. Use a spatula to scramble the eggs in the pan. Scrape along the bottom of the pan in all directions to keep the eggs moving.

If the pan is sufficiently pre-heated, the eggs will be set quickly, in about 60 seconds. Serve immediately.

Variation:

To jazz up your scrambled eggs, you can mix in some vegetables, roasted potatoes, and/or cheese while the eggs are cooking. Fresh herbs can be mixed in as well. For a Mexican twist, mix in cooked beans, salsa, and cheese. Wrap it up in a warm tortilla for a breakfast burrito.

Warning

Scrambled eggs get cold very quickly. Make sure the table is set, drinks are poured, and toast is toasted before you start cooking the eggs. Serve them immediately after cooking them, or else keep them warm in a covered dish in the oven until ready to serve.

BOILED EGGS. This is another way to cook a big batch all at one time. They can be made ahead of time and eaten as part of a quick, no prep breakfast on a busy morning. Boiled eggs also make an easy snack, and they can be chopped up into an egg salad. Some people prefer soft-boiled eggs, while others like hard-boiled eggs. Either way, they're simple to make.

Yield: 4 servings　　　　　　*Prep Time: 5 minutes*
Serving Size: 2 eggs　　　　　*Cook Time: varies*

Ingredients:
8 large eggs in their shells

Directions:
1.　In a medium pot, boil enough water to cover the eggs by at least one inch. When the water comes to a boil, reduce the heat so you have a low simmer (just barely bubbling). If the water is bubbling too much, you'll risk cracking the eggs when you place them in the pot.

2. Carefully lower the eggs one at a time into the simmering water. I like to use a slotted spoon to lower each egg into the water, but you can also get a special basket that safely lowers eggs into the water for boiling.

3. To make soft boiled eggs, simmer for 6 minutes if the eggs are starting cold from the refrigerator. If the eggs are starting at room temperature, the cooking time can be reduced to 4 minutes. After simmering the eggs for the appointed time, remove them from the pot. Gently cut the shells off the top third of the pointier end of the eggs with a knife. Scoop the eggs into small bowls and serve.

4. To make hard boiled eggs, simmer for 18 minutes (or 16 minutes if they're starting at room temperature). After cooking, remove the eggs from the water and submerge them in a bowl of cold water. Once they're ready to handle, you can peel them. Tap each egg on the counter, then roll it along the counter while pressing gently. This should allow you to remove the peel easily. Rinse the eggs before serving to avoid leaving any little bits of shell on them.

FRIED EGGS. Fried eggs are a great breakfast for a weekend morning. These take a little longer to prepare because the eggs are cooked to order for each person. In my family of four, our fried egg preferences run the gamut from over easy to over medium to over hard. Once you get experienced at this, you can cook two eggs at a time in the pan. Fried eggs are wonderful with toast and fruit, and below the recipe is a fun variation that kids love.

Yield: 4 servings   *Prep Time: 5 minutes*
Serving Size: 2 eggs   *Cook Time: 10 minutes*

Ingredients:
8 eggs   Salt and pepper
1 tbsp. butter

Directions:
Heat a large skillet over medium heat for a minute. Add the butter and melt it over medium heat. Crack an egg into a glass or small bowl.

Over Easy: For an over easy egg, pour the egg into the hot pan. Cook the egg for 1-2 minutes, or until the white is set. Then flip it quickly with a spatula large enough to manage the size of the egg. If you're tentative while flipping, the whole egg won't flip neatly and you'll have a bit of a mess in the pan. It's okay, though. It's still perfectly edible – it just won't look as pretty. After flipping, cook for another 15 seconds.
Over Medium: Proceed as directed above for over easy eggs, but let the second side cook for 30 seconds, or until the desired consistency is reached.
Over Hard: Proceed as directed above for over easy eggs, but let the second side cook for a minute or more, until the desired consistency is reached. For over hard eggs, you may want to break

the yolk with the corner of the spatula while it's cooking to distribute the yolk across the egg.

Best Way to Crack Eggs

If you crack an egg directly into a pan or a mixing bowl with other ingredients, you risk getting bits of eggshell where you don't want them. It's tricky to remove eggshell pieces from a cooking egg in a pan or a mixing bowl full of cookie dough ingredients. To avoid this hassle, always crack eggs into their own little bowl first. That way, you can easily remove stray eggshell pieces with a spoon without having to deal with complications.

Variation:

Egg in a Hole. This is a fun way to serve an egg, and it's a bit easier to flip the egg this way. Toast a piece of bread, then use a small glass or cookie cutter (2½- to 3- inch diameter) to cut a hole in the center of the toast. Put the outer portion of the toast in a heated, buttered pan on the stovetop. Crack an egg into a small glass or bowl, then pour it into the open space in the middle of the toast. Cook over medium for about 30 seconds, then flip the toast and egg together in one swift flip. Cook on the other side for another 60 seconds, or until the desired consistency is reached. Serve immediately.

BREAKFAST CASSEROLE. An egg-based breakfast casserole is a great make-ahead breakfast for feeding a crowd. It includes protein, whole grains, calcium, and even a green vegetable. What more could you want in the morning? You can prepare the ingredients the night before, and then assemble the casserole in the morning and put it in the oven. Bring this casserole to a brunch for a hearty, flavorful addition to the food spread.

Yield: 9 servings　　　　　　　*Prep Time: 20 minutes*
Serving Size: 3 x 4 inch piece　　*Cook Time: 45 minutes*

Ingredients:

2 cups whole wheat bread cubes

1 cup asparagus, chopped into 1-inch pieces (discard tough stems)

12 eggs

6 ounces breakfast sausage or bacon, cooked and broken into bite-sized pieces

1 cup plain yogurt

1 tsp. mustard powder

1½ tsp. salt

2 tbsp. diced scallions

Directions:

1. Preheat the oven to 325 degrees. Grease a 9 by 13 inch pan and boil a small pot of water.
2. Spread the bread cubes evenly in the bottom of the baking pan.
3. Place the asparagus pieces in the water for one minute. Check to see if they're tender by piercing a piece of asparagus with a fork. If they're still quite hard, give them another minute in the water. Once the asparagus is just tender, place the pieces in the baking dish on top of the bread.
4. Add the chopped sausage or bacon to the baking dish.

5. In a large bowl, whisk together the eggs, yogurt, mustard powder, and salt until you have a uniform yellow color. Pour the mixture into the baking dish.
6. Sprinkle the scallions on top.
7. Bake for about 45 minutes, until the eggs are set. They should no longer be liquid-y at all. Serve warm.

"This is a great and easy recipe to make. It's very versatile and you can change the veggie to whatever your family likes!" ~ Becca

Whole Grain Weekend Breakfast

It's such a treat to have a long, leisurely breakfast at least once a week. Food is meant to be savored and enjoyed. Family life can get so hectic sometimes, and mealtimes can get rushed or forgotten. Still, we need to carve out time to sit and enjoy food with our loved ones. For my family, this happens on the weekends. Groggy family members, baked breakfast goodies, and maple syrup often come together around our kitchen table on a Saturday morning.

Pancakes, waffles, and French toast are some of our favorite weekend breakfast foods. These are traditionally made with white flour, but we use whole grains to make them. If your family is hesitant to eat food made from whole wheat flour, pancakes and waffles are the perfect place to start adding more whole grains into their diets. Who doesn't love a plate of food that's covered with maple syrup?

If you're just starting out with whole grains, you can substitute unbleached, all-purpose white flour for a third of the white whole wheat flour in these recipes. Over time, cut back on the amount of all-purpose flour until you're using all whole wheat flour.

There are three main categories of whole wheat flour: traditional whole wheat flour, white whole wheat flour, and whole wheat pastry flour. All these categories are whole grain, meaning they include the entire wheat stalk (germ, bran, and endosperm). They're all more nutritious than all-purpose white flour, which only contains the endosperm of the wheat stalk.

I recommend experimenting with these three types of whole wheat flour to see which one your family likes best. My family prefers white whole wheat flour and whole wheat pastry flour because they're a bit lighter in texture than plain whole wheat flour.

Whole wheat flour should be stored in the refrigerator or freezer. Because it's less processed than all-purpose white flour, it contains oils from the germ that can be negatively impacted by heat or light. Place your flour in an airtight container for up to 6 months in the refrigerator or freezer. In the winter months, it's okay to store whole wheat flour in a dry, cool pantry for up to three months.

PANCAKES. Pancakes are the classic weekend breakfast treat. Serve them with a side of fruit for a nutritious morning meal. Pancakes are lower in protein than some other breakfast options, so you may want to add chopped nuts or a side of bacon to help keep you full until lunchtime.

Traditional pancakes use milk and melted butter as the liquid ingredients. My family prefers yogurt-based pancakes, though, because they're lighter and fluffier than traditional pancakes. You can make the batter the night before and store it in an airtight container in the refrigerator. I adapted this recipe from one of my favorite cookbooks, *Joy of Cooking*.

Yield: 12 3-inch pancakes   *Prep Time: 10 minutes*
Serving Size: 3 pancakes   *Cook Time: 10 minutes*

Ingredients:

1 ½ cups white whole wheat
    flour
1 tbsp. sugar or maple syrup
¾ tsp. salt

¾ tsp. baking soda
3 eggs
1 ½ cup plain whole milk
    yogurt

Directions:

1. Preheat the griddle to 375 degrees and preheat the oven to 170 degrees.
2. In a small bowl, stir together the flour, sugar, salt, and baking soda.
3. Crack the eggs into a large bowl. Stir briskly with a fork to mix together the yolk and the egg white. Stir in the yogurt.
4. Add the dry ingredients to the wet ingredients and stir until just combined. It's okay to have a few small lumps. If you mix the batter until it's perfectly smooth, the pancakes won't come out as fluffy as they could.
5. Pour the batter onto the hot, greased griddle in 3-inch circles. Cook for about 1½ minutes, then use a spatula to lift a pancake slightly. Look at the bottom and see if it's lightly browned. If so, flip the pancakes using a brisk, definitive motion. If you flip tentatively, it won't be pretty (but of course you can still eat it).
6. Cook the pancakes on the other side for about 1½ minutes. Remove one pancake and poke a hole in the middle to see if it's cooked through. These pancakes should be quite moist in the middle, but the batter shouldn't still be raw.
7. When you remove a batch of pancakes from the griddle, transfer them to a covered casserole dish and place them in the warm oven. That way, everyone can eat together once all the pancakes are cooked.

Serve with pure maple syrup and fruit.

Substituting Gluten-Free Flour

If someone in your family has a gluten allergy or intolerance, you can easily substitute gluten-free flour for whole wheat flour. In most instances, you can replace the whole wheat flour with an equal amount of gluten-free flour (see page 219 for my gluten-free flour recipe). However, whole wheat flour tends to be a bit "thirstier" than gluten-free flour or all-purpose white flour. So if you're using gluten-free flour in a recipe that calls for whole wheat flour, you may want use a little less liquid by eliminating 1 or 2 tablespoons of the liquid ingredients for every cup of flour.

WAFFLES. On birthdays and other special occasions, we like to have waffles for breakfast. Since they're made one at a time, they take a bit longer to prepare than a batch of pancakes. Serve them with fruit and a side of bacon or sausage if desired. You can make them extra special by adding decadent toppings like whipped cream (page 212), berry sauce, or chocolate sauce. These freeze well, so you may want to double the batch and pull them out of the freezer for a special weekday treat.

Yield: 6, 7-inch waffles　　　*Prep Time: 10 minutes*
Serving Size: 1½ waffles　　　*Cook Time: 20 minutes*

Ingredients:

2 cups white whole wheat
    flour
1 tbsp. baking powder
½ tsp. salt

3 eggs
1½ cups milk
½ cup melted butter
2 tsp. vanilla extract

Directions:

1. Preheat the oven to 170 degrees and preheat a waffle iron.
2. In a small bowl, stir together the flour, baking powder, and salt.
3. In a large bowl, mix the eggs, milk, butter, and vanilla extract. Add the dry ingredients to the wet ingredients and stir to just combine. If the batter is very thick, add a few extra tablespoons of milk to get a thick but pourable consistency.
4. Scoop a ladleful of batter onto a hot waffle iron and cook until light brown. Repeat with the remaining batter.
5. As you make the waffles, place them in the oven to keep them warm. You can put them directly on the oven racks or place them in a large casserole dish. Keep them warm until they're all cooked, then everyone can eat together.

You can freeze any leftover waffles after you cook them. Let them cool completely, then freeze them in a zipper bag or large, airtight container. When you're ready to serve the waffles, heat them up in the oven at 350 degrees for 5 to 10 minutes or until fully defrosted.

TRADITIONAL FRENCH TOAST. With whole grain bread and lots of eggs, French toast is a nice hybrid breakfast treat. Traditional French toast is made by dipping individual slices of bread into a mixture of milk and eggs, and then cooking them in a pan or on a griddle. This is a great way to salvage bread that's going stale.

Yield: 8 slices   *Prep Time: 5 minutes*
Serving Size: 2 slices   *Cook Time: 20 minutes*

Ingredients:
4 eggs   ½ tsp. cinnamon
1 cup milk   1 tbsp. butter
2 tbsp. maple syrup   8 slices whole grain bread
1 tsp. vanilla extract

Directions:
1. Preheat the oven to 170 degrees if you don't have a large enough griddle to cook all the French toast at once. You'll be keeping the first pieces warm in the oven while you cook the rest of the batch.
2. In a medium bowl, stir together the eggs, milk, maple syrup, vanilla extract, and cinnamon.
3. In a medium skillet, melt the butter over medium heat. Turn the heat down to medium low.
4. Dip a piece of bread into the egg mixture. Let it soak for several seconds so it gets saturated.
5. Carefully transfer the bread to the skillet. Cook the bread for about a minute on each side, until well browned. Poke the center of the French toast with the corner of a spatula to peek inside and see if it's cooked through. It should be moist, but not very mushy.

6. Repeat with the remaining slices of bread. As each piece is cooked, place it in a covered casserole dish in the warm oven so everyone can eat together.
7. If you still have some of the egg mixture left after making 8 pieces of French toast, you can continue with more pieces of bread until the egg mixture is gone.

Serve warm with maple syrup and fruit.

FRENCH TOAST CASSEROLE. French toast has more protein than pancakes or waffles because of all the eggs and milk, but you still get to reach for the maple syrup jug. If you want to take a shortcut, you can bake a French toast casserole in the oven. This is a great make-ahead option.

Yield: 9 servings *Prep Time: 10 minutes*
Serving Size: 3 x 4 inch piece *Cook Time: 30 minutes*

Ingredients:
12 cups whole grain bread, cut into 2-inch squares
8 eggs
1½ cups whole milk

3 tbsp. maple syrup
½ tsp. cinnamon
2 tsp. vanilla extract

Directions:
1. Cut the bread into 2-inch square pieces. Place them in a 9 by 13 inch pan.
2. In a medium bowl, beat the eggs and stir in the milk, syrup, cinnamon, and vanilla. Pour this mixture over the bread. Use your hands to move the bread pieces around in the egg mixture so each piece gets soaked.

3. Cover the baking dish with foil and refrigerate overnight. If you're preparing this dish in the morning, let it sit for at least 30 minutes before baking.
4. In the morning, preheat the oven to 375 degrees.
5. Bake the casserole, covered, for about 30 minutes. Check to see if it's set. If the casserole is still watery or the bread pieces are very wet and mushy, cook uncovered for another five minutes (or until set). The final product should be moist but not overly mushy. Don't bake it too long or it will be dry.

Serve warm with fruit and maple syrup.

Yogurt Treats

Yogurt is a highly nutritious food to include at breakfast time. Full of protein, calcium, and other vitamins and minerals, yogurt will help you to stay full through the morning. More importantly, it's full of probiotics, the good bacteria that your digestive tract needs to do its work.

At my grocery store, the yogurt section is massive. There are so many different brands and flavors to choose from that it can be tricky to know where to start. I'll make it easy for you. The only yogurt I recommend purchasing is plain, whole milk yogurt with live, active cultures. This yogurt is less processed than low-fat or fat-free yogurt, and it contains fats that are essential to good health. In addition, when fat is removed from yogurt, the taste suffers. As a result, lots of sugar and chemicals are added to low-fat yogurt to bring back the flavor that was lost when the fat was removed. Plain, whole milk yogurt contains nearly twice the protein of sweetened, fat-free yogurt.

Sadly, most yogurt you'll find at the grocery store these days is highly sweetened low-fat or fat-free yogurt. A small, 6-ounce container of a popular brand's fat-free Strawberry Yogurt includes modified corn starch, artificial food coloring, and 26 grams of sugar. This is more than two-thirds of the daily amount of added sugar recommended for women by the American Heart Association. Twenty-six grams of sugar is the amount found in two frosted toaster pastries or four chocolate cream-filled cookies. If you want to start your day with that much sugar, I recommend the cookies instead of the yogurt. At least you won't walk out of the house thinking you've just started your day with something healthy.

Why Minimize Sugar in Your Diet

A diet high in sugar can be harmful to your physical and mental health. Sugar intake increases the acidity in your body, increasing the risk of illness, inflammation, and obesity. In addition, research indicates that high sugar consumption heightens the risk of depression and exacerbates the symptoms of anxiety.

My family eats lots of yogurt, and I was so happy to discover a few years ago that it's simple to make your own yogurt at home. If you're just starting out on your homemade food journey and this sounds a little wacky to you, keep it in the back of your mind. Down the road when you're ready, check out my recipe for homemade yogurt on page 215. It takes less than 10 minutes of hands-on time, and it tastes amazing. It also costs four times less than the store-bought version.

YOGURT PARFAIT. A yogurt parfait is a refreshing breakfast for a busy morning. It includes the nutritional benefits of whole milk yogurt, plus fresh fruit and whole grains from the granola. For those who don't like the distinct flavor of plain yogurt, this recipe includes a bit of maple syrup and vanilla extract to sweeten the deal. You can also flavor plain yogurt with puréed berries, lemon extract, or other fruit.

This yogurt parfait is a delicious breakfast treat that can be assembled in minutes.

Yield: 4 servings   *Prep Time: 5 minutes*
Serving Size: 1 cup

Ingredients:

2½ cups plain, whole milk   1½ tsp. vanilla extract
     yogurt   1¼ cup granola (p. 78)
1 tbsp. maple syrup or honey   ¼ cup berries
     (or to taste)

Directions:

1. In a large bowl, stir together the yogurt, maple syrup or honey, and vanilla extract.
2. Prepare four 1-cup glasses or parfait bowls. Stack the ingredients evenly among the four bowls as follows: yogurt on the bottom, then granola, then fruit. Repeat this pattern with a second layer of yogurt, then granola, then fruit.

Serve immediately. Alternately, store sweetened yogurt and berries in separate containers in the refrigerator. Assemble the parfaits when you're ready to serve them.

SMOOTHIES. If you're someone who isn't especially hungry in the morning, a yogurt smoothie might be just what you need for breakfast. Smoothies are also a great way to add some nutrients to a small breakfast like toast with peanut butter. You can hide just about anything in a smoothie, so you may be able to get some extra fruits and vegetables into your picky eater with a smoothie. I'm including two smoothie combinations below, but the possibilities are endless. Experiment with ingredients you like. For those with dairy sensitivities, you can make smoothies with non-dairy milk, or skip the milk altogether and just use fruits and vegetables.

Fruit Smoothie

Yield: 4 servings   *Prep Time: 5 minutes*
Serving Size: 1 cup

Ingredients:
2 cups mango chunks   1 cup milk
1 medium banana   3 tbsp. honey, or to taste
1¼ cup plain yogurt

Directions:
Place all the ingredients in a blender and mix until well-combined and smooth.

Taste the smoothie and adjust the flavors as needed. You may want more mango or more honey, depending on how sweet your bananas are.

Cooking With Yogurt

If you heat yogurt at a high temp., some of the beneficial bacteria will be destroyed. It's not harmful to eat yogurt that's been baked into muffins or pancakes, but it isn't as nutritious as cold yogurt. Include smoothies and yogurt parfaits in your diet regularly to give your gut the full advantage of yogurt's helpful bacteria.

Green Smoothie

Yield: 4 servings   *Serving Size: 1 cup*
Prep Time: 5 minutes

Ingredients:

1 cup full-fat coconut milk (or whole milk)

1 cup water

¼ cup frozen spinach or ¼ lb. fresh chopped spinach (or more, to taste)

1½ cups strawberries, chopped

2 medium ripe bananas

2 tbsp. cooked or soaked oatmeal

Directions:

Place all the ingredients in a blender and purée until smooth. Taste the smoothie to see if it needs a bit of maple syrup for extra sweetness.

Divide into 4 glasses and serve.

It's important to start your day with a variety of nutritious foods for breakfast. Use the recipes here as a starting point for your breakfast meal plans. Once you master these basic recipes, you can find other fun breakfast ideas in magazines, in cookbooks, and on the web. By providing your family with a healthy breakfast each morning, you're giving them the tools they need to navigate their day.

Chapter Five
Snack Time

Getting from one meal to the next without eating can be difficult for some of us. Everyone has a unique metabolism, and mine happens to run on overdrive. No matter how much I eat for lunch, I'm always hungry well before dinnertime. I get weak and downright cranky until I have a chance to eat something. The hungrier I get, the lower my standards become. I just want to put something – anything – in my stomach to make it stop growling at me.

This really isn't the best approach to snack time. Snacks should be productive, giving your body fuel to function at its best. Healthy snacks help keep your blood sugar levels stable, and they contribute to a positive mood and energy level. Junk food may taste good and fill your stomach temporarily, but it isn't productive. Good snacks add value– they don't just silence your growling stomach. They include things like whole grains, fiber, vitamins, minerals, and protein.

The challenge at snack time is being able to get your hands on something productive to eat. Unlike breakfast, lunch, and dinner, snack time isn't usually a planned out, sit-down occasion. Snacks are often eaten while you're doing other things. With advanced preparation, it isn't difficult to eat productive snacks. This chapter outlines several types of snacks you can stock up on at home. They're easily portable so you can take them with you when you leave the house in the morning.

Nuts About Nuts

Nuts are one of the most efficient snacks you'll find. Rich in protein, fiber, and omega-3 fatty acids, they can be effective in tiding you over until your next meal. They're good for your brain and your heart, and they can help prevent disease. Each type of nut has unique health benefits, so it's good to eat a variety. I like to keep peanuts, almonds, hazelnuts, pistachio nuts, and walnuts in my pantry.

As with many other healthy foods, nuts have been degraded by the processed food industry. Many options in the nut aisle at the grocery store include lengthy ingredient lists full of unnecessary additives. This is another example of how you're better off buying foods as close to their natural state as possible. For example, a popular brand's dry roasted peanuts list 13 ingredients, including gelatin, corn starch, corn syrup, and maltodextrin. Who wants corn on their peanuts? Sweetened nuts are even worse, sometimes containing as much added sugar per serving as a pastry.

When shopping for nuts, look for raw or dry-roasted nuts that have no ingredients other than nuts and perhaps salt. This same principle holds true for nut butters. The sweetened peanut butter of my childhood holds fond memories, but I don't buy it for my family. We eat peanut butter that has nothing but peanuts in it.

Each of my grocery stores has at least one version of single-ingredient peanut butter on the shelf, so it isn't hard to find. Other nut butters, such as almond and cashew butter, tend to be more expensive than peanut butter, but they're good options as well.

Storing Nuts

Nuts can typically be stored at room temperature for at least three months. To extend their shelf life, you can store nuts in the refrigerator for up to six months or in the freezer for up to a year.

Homemade trail mix makes a quick snack that's popular with kids and adults. Just combine a variety of nuts with raisins and a few chocolate chips in a zipper bag. You can take this with you on a hike or an afternoon of errands. This is a good "emergency snack" that you can store in your glove compartment during the cooler months for family members who get cranky when they need to eat.

Keeping rice cakes on hand gives you a base for a nut butter snack. Rather than eating yet another piece of bread, try a single-ingredient brown rice cake with peanut butter and fresh fruit for a snack.

Protein Bars

Unlike the packaged granola bars you find at the grocery store, homemade energy bars can be very nutritious. In general, it's best to keep the sweetener to a minimum while maximizing the protein and grains. Dried fruit is a great substitute for added sugar in these bars.

RAW ENERGY BARS. My favorite snack of all is a homemade Larabar. These raw energy bars are made primarily from nuts and dates, with a few other healthy flavor additions. There are so many different variations you can make, and I'm including two of my favorites here. You can substitute other nuts according to your preferences, and play with the proportions.

Chocolate Energy Bars

Yield: 8 bars   *Prep Time: 10 minutes*
Serving Size: 1 x 5 inch bar

Ingredients:

1½ cups Medjool dates   2 tbsp. cocoa powder
1½ cups cashews or other   ¼ cup shredded coconut
   nuts   1 to 2 tsp. water, if needed

Directions:

1. Place all the ingredients except the water in a food processor and process for 1 to 2 minutes. You want to see some small chunks of all the different ingredients, so don't mix for so long that it becomes a uniform paste.
2. Test to see if the mixture binds easily. If it's still a little crumbly, add water one teaspoon at a time until it binds together easily. If you accidentally add too much water, add a few extra nuts or a little dried coconut.
3. Transfer the mixture to a 9 by 5 inch pan or storage container and press down with your fingers to make it level. If you want thicker bars, you can use a smaller container.
4. Cover and refrigerate for an hour, and then cut into 8 bars.

5. Transfer the bars to an airtight container and refrigerate. These bars can be frozen as well.

Apple Pie Energy Bars

Yield: 8 bars   *Prep Time: 10 minutes*
Serving Size: 1 x 5 inch bar

Ingredients:

1½ cups walnuts   ¼ tsp. cinnamon
1 cup dried apples   ⅛ tsp. ginger
1 cup Medjool dates, pits   ⅛ tsp. salt
   removed

Directions:

1. In a food processor, combine all the ingredients and chop them until a paste is formed. Don't chop them so much that you can't see little bits of walnuts, apples, and dates.
2. Test to see if the mixture binds together easily. If it's crumbly, add water one teaspoon at a time until it binds together. If you accidentally add too much water, add a few extra nuts or some extra dried apple.
3. Transfer the mixture to a 9 by 5 inch pan or storage container and press down with your fingers to make it level.
4. Cover and refrigerate for an hour, and then cut into 8 bars.
5. Transfer the bars to an airtight container and refrigerate.

Variation: These energy bars can be formed into other shapes, too. You can cut them into small squares instead of rectangular bars. Also, if you're in a hurry you can shape the mixture into 1-inch balls. They'll set more quickly in the refrigerator this way.

Nature's Candy

Medjool dates are known as "nature's candy." They add sweetness to many different types of dishes. Even if you don't like them plain, they can add sweet flavor and dimension to brownies, protein bars, and smoothies. You can also use them to sweeten homemade nut butters, granola, or truffles. Even though they're sweet like sugar, dates are more nutritious because they contain fiber and antioxidants.

BAKED GRANOLA BARS. Fresh baked granola bars are a delicious snack, and they smell amazing while they're baking in the oven. These are a good source of whole grains and nuts. They taste more like a treat than some other snacks, so they're a good option for kids who are getting adjusted to the transition from packaged food to homemade food.

Yield: 14 bars
Serving Size: 2 x 4 inch bar

Prep Time: 15 minutes
Cook Time: 25 minutes

Ingredients:
1 cup white whole wheat flour
½ tsp. cinnamon
½ tsp. baking powder
¼ tsp. salt
⅔ cup melted butter or coconut oil
⅔ cup pure maple syrup
1 egg
1 tsp. vanilla extract

2 cups rolled oats
1 cup unsweetened shredded coconut
1 cup finely chopped nuts (e.g. walnuts, almonds, hazelnuts)
1½ cups dried fruit (e.g. apricots, raisins, dried cranberries)
½ cup chocolate chips (opt.)

Directions:
1. Grease a 9 by 13 inch pan with butter or oil and preheat the oven to 350 degrees.
2. In a small bowl, combine the flour, cinnamon, baking powder, and salt.
3. In a large bowl, mix together the melted butter or oil, syrup, egg, and vanilla. Stir in the flour mixture until combined.
4. Add the oats, coconut, nuts, and dried fruit, and stir to combine.
5. Press the dough evenly into the 9 by 13 inch pan. Press down any pieces of dried fruit so they're not right on top (they may burn up there). Bake on the center rack in the oven for 20 to 25 minutes, until the edges are beginning to get brown.
6. Cool completely on a wire rack and cut into 14 bars. If you try to cut them before they're completely cool, they'll likely crumble apart. I know they smell amazing, but hang in there and wait until they're cool.

Store the bars in an airtight container for up to four days. You can also freeze them for several months.

> "I have never made granola bars before and loved how simple the recipe is and how it is open to a variety of different fruit and nuts. This is a winner in my book." ~ Rachel

Chickpea Goodies

Chickpeas are ancient legumes that have been nourishing societies for thousands of years. Also known as garbanzo beans, this staple of Indian cuisine has become popular in many other countries as well. Chickpeas are high in protein, fiber, iron, and folate. A half cup of cooked chickpeas has about seven grams of protein, which is more than many other snack options. These are great to add to your snack rotation.

You can purchase chickpeas in a can, but I prefer to make them myself. They cost $.17 per cup when you start with dried garbanzo beans, but they're $.50 or more per cup when you buy the canned version. Also, canned chickpeas often contain preservatives and high sodium levels.

To cook dried chickpeas, soak them for at least eight hours (or overnight) in a big pot of water. They'll double in size after soaking. Drain and rinse the chickpeas, then return them to the pot. Add enough water to cover the chickpeas by at least two inches, and bring to a boil.

Lower the heat and simmer for 1 to 2 hours, depending on how tender you want them. For hummus, you'll want them to be quite tender. For roasted chickpeas, soups, or salads, they can be a bit more firm.

SAVORY ROASTED CHICKPEAS. Roasted chickpeas make a delicious, high-protein snack that's easy to make at home. Many of us crave something salty between meals, but potato chips and pretzels don't provide much nutrition. This is the perfect alternative.

Roasted chickpeas are high in protein and deliciously addictive.

Yield: 1½ cups   *Prep Time: 5 minutes*
Serving Size: ½ cup   *Cook Time: 40 minutes*

Ingredients:
2 cups cooked chickpeas   ¼ tsp. chili powder
1 tsp. salt   ¼ tsp. cayenne pepper (or to
¾ tsp. smoked paprika   taste)

Directions:

1. Preheat the oven to 400 degrees.
2. Stir together the seasonings in a small bowl. Pour most of the seasoning over the chickpeas in a large bowl and stir to coat evenly. If your chickpeas aren't moist enough for the seasoning to stick, you may want to stir in a ½ teaspoon of melted butter or oil to help bind the spices to the chickpeas. Taste a chickpea, and see if the flavoring is as strong as you'd like it. Add the remainder of the seasoning if desired.
3. Place the chickpeas in a single layer in a roasting pan or on a cookie sheet with sides.
4. Bake for 35 to 40 minutes, stirring every 10 minutes.

These can be stored in an airtight container at room temperature. They'll keep for several days, but you may want to put them under the broiler for a minute or two to make them crispy if they've lost their crunch.

Variation:

For a sweet version of roasted chickpeas, coat 2 cups of cooked chickpeas with 2 tablespoons of maple syrup, ¼ teaspoon cinnamon, and ⅛ teaspoon ginger. Bake as directed above.

Warning!

Be very careful when using the broiler in your oven. It's a great tool for quickly melting or browning food, but it gets very hot. If you walk away from the oven with the broiler on, you could have flames shooting out of your oven within minutes (I say from experience). Keep peeking in the oven every 20 seconds or so to be sure you know what's going on in there.

HUMMUS. Hummus is a delicious chickpea-based dip or spread that's perfect for snack time. Carrots, cucumbers, and red pepper strips taste great with a little hummus. There are many varieties of pre-made hummus at the grocery store, but you're better off making your own. Store-bought hummus can cost about four times as much as the homemade version, and it's often full of unnecessary additives. It only takes a few minutes to whip up a batch of homemade hummus in your blender or food processor.

Yield: 2 cups   *Prep Time: 10 minutes*
Serving Size: 2 tablespoons

Ingredients:

2 cups cooked chickpeas

3 tbsp. tahini (sesame seed paste)

2 tbsp. lemon juice

¼ cup olive oil

1 small clove garlic, puréed (or more, to taste)

¾ tsp. salt

¼ cup water

Directions:

1. In a food processor or blender, combine the chickpeas, tahini, lemon juice, garlic, salt, and olive oil. Process for about 20 seconds, then add half the water.
2. Continue to process until smooth. Add the remaining water if needed to make your hummus a spreadable consistency.
3. If it's too thick, add additional water one teaspoon at a time until you have a creamy consistency. If it's too thin, you can add more chickpeas. Taste the hummus and adjust the salt if needed.
    Store the hummus in an airtight container in the refrigerator.

Variations: If you take a look at the hummus shelf at your grocery store, you'll notice that there are a million and one ways to flavor hummus. The recipe here is a basic version, and you can add different vegetables or herbs to change the flavor. I like adding a few sun-dried tomatoes and some scallions or chives to my hummus. Experiment with different add-ins to come up with your favorite combination. Also, if you don't have tahini, you can still make hummus. Just add a little extra water and olive oil to make up for the lack of tahini.

Tip

Even with a high-quality food processor, garlic can be tricky to purée. To avoid having little bits of garlic in your hummus, I recommend puréeing it before adding it to the food processor. Use a microplane or a mortar and pestle to pulverize the little guy.

Popcorn Power

Popcorn is one of the easiest whole grain snacks to put together on a moment's notice. I panic when I run out of popcorn kernels. If I end up hosting a last-minute playdate and my pantry is empty, at least I know that I can always pop popcorn. Most children love it, so it's a safe bet for snack time. It's not exactly a power snack, but popcorn *is* a whole grain, and it goes nicely with a side of fruit. It's also a fun treat for a family movie night.

I recommend making popcorn with an air popper and then seasoning it yourself. Flavored popcorn that's already popped can be found in bags in the snack aisle at the grocery store, but these aren't a great choice. They're much more expensive than home-popped popcorn, and they tend to include preservatives. Microwave popcorn is even worse because it typically includes chemical flavorings and hydrogenated oils. Many packages of "butter-flavored" microwave popcorn don't even contain butter in their ingredient lists.

To make popcorn in an air popper, follow the manufacturer's instructions for your machine. Most machines have a capacity for half a cup of popcorn kernels per batch. This yields about 15 cups of popcorn.

If you don't have an air popper, you can pop popcorn on the stovetop. To do this, melt two tablespoons of coconut oil in a large covered pan over medium heat. Place 3 popcorn kernels in the pan, cover, and wait to hear that first pop. Then add half a cup of kernels to the pan in a single layer. Cover the pan and jostle it periodically so the popcorn doesn't burn. Listen to the popping, and when it slows down, turn off the burner. Wait until the popping stops completely, and carefully remove the lid. Sometimes you'll get a late pop at this point, so you may need to shield yourself with the lid.

MAPLE POPCORN. This sweet homemade snack is deliciously addictive. The cinnamon-ginger combination makes it taste like candy, but it's healthier for you. This is a great way to satisfy your sweet tooth.

Yield: 12 cups   *Prep Time: 5 minutes*
Serving Size: 3 cups   *Cook Time: 10 minutes*

Ingredients:
½ cup popcorn kernels   3 tbsp. maple syrup
(generates 15 cups popped)   ½ tsp. ground ginger
3 tbsp. melted butter or   ½ tsp. cinnamon
coconut oil   ¼ tsp. salt

Directions:
1. Preheat the oven to 325 degrees.
2. Pop the popcorn using an air popper.

3. Place the butter or coconut oil in a large roasting pan with sides. Put the pan in the oven until the butter or oil melts.
4. Remove the pan from the oven and add the maple syrup and seasonings. Stir to combine the toppings right in the pan. This saves you from having to wash an extra bowl.
5. Add the popped popcorn to the pan and stir it so that the popcorn is evenly coated.
6. Bake for 6 to 8 minutes, stirring every couple minutes. Once it starts to brown a little, it's done.

Remove and cool on a wire rack.

SAVORY FIESTA POPCORN. Try this savory popcorn when you're in the mood for a salty snack. The taco seasoning tastes delicious on popcorn. This is a great snack to put in a big bowl when you're entertaining a crowd.

Yield: 12 cups   *Prep Time: 5 minutes*
Serving Size: 3 cups   *Cook Time: 10 minutes*

Ingredients:
½ cup organic popcorn kernels
3 tbsp. melted butter or

coconut oil
1½ tsp. taco seasoning (page 222)

Directions:
1. Preheat the oven to 325 degrees.
2. Pop the popcorn kernels in an air popper.
3. Place the butter or coconut oil in a large roasting pan with sides. Put the pan in the oven until the butter or oil melts.
4. Then sprinkle the taco seasoning into the melted butter or oil.
5. Add the popped popcorn to the roasting pan and stir to coat the popcorn evenly with the topping.

6.   Bake for 6 to 8 minutes, stirring every couple minutes.

Remove and cool on a wire rack. Store the popcorn in an airtight container.

Muffins and Breads

Muffins and breads are another type of nutritious snack. I'm not talking about the sugar-coated, crumb topping muffins you find in the case at the coffee shop. Those are dessert. You can make muffins at home that are delicious, fairly nutritious, and less sugar-laden than the goodies at the bakery. When we focus on whole grains and fruits or vegetables in muffins, we bring productive ingredients to the table.

Bread to Muffins Conversion

If you find a recipe for banana bread but you really want banana muffins, it's not a problem. Bread and muffin recipes can be used interchangeably, and the only thing you need to adapt is the baking time. Mini muffins take about 15 minutes to bake, and regular muffins take 20 to 25 minutes. Mini bread loaves take 30 to 40 minutes, and regular bread loaves take 40 to 60 minutes. Start checking them on the early end of the time window, because heat levels can vary from one oven to the next.

During the summer, I get lots of fresh produce from my farm share. I also stock up on seasonal fruits and vegetables at the farmers' market and the grocery store. I love to buy way too much of these things so that I can stash some away in the freezer. Grated carrots and zucchini are perfect for muffins. Berries, rhubarb, and peaches can be baked into goodies as well.

Some people believe that cooking or baking produce always minimizes its nutrients, but this isn't true. In some cases, nutrients do suffer when food is cooked. But in other cases, nutrients can be more readily absorbed by the body when foods are eaten in cooked form. In my opinion, there's nothing wrong with eating your carrots in a muffin once in a while.

Many recipes for muffins and breads use white, all-purpose flour. I suggest substituting at least half whole wheat flour for some of the white flour. A white flour muffin isn't a productive snack in the way that a whole wheat flour muffin is. By using the whole grain, you include more fiber and protein in your snack.

Also, typical muffin recipes use a lot more sugar than they need. Try cutting a third or more of the sugar out of a traditional recipe. You'll probably find that it's plenty sweet enough. As you move away from overly sweetened processed food, your taste buds will come to prefer a more subtle amount of sweetness in baked goods, and the taste of a bakery muffin may make you cringe.

Definition: Blueberries

Wild blueberries and cultivated blueberries are both wonderful summertime treats. Wild blueberries are the small, pea-sized berries found in the freezer section at the grocery store. Native to Maine and Canada, they have a more concentrated flavor and a higher antioxidant level than the larger, cultivated blueberries found in the produce section. I prefer wild blueberries for baking because of their smaller size and stronger flavor.

LEMON BLUEBERRY MUFFINS. Blueberries and lemons make a wonderful flavor combination. These delicious muffins are a sweet treat that you can enjoy with your coffee or tea in the morning. They're also a great addition to a school lunch box. I love to stock up on blueberries in the summer so I can make these muffins any time of year.

Yield: 12 muffins

Prep Time: 10 minutes

Serving Size: one muffin

Cook Time: 20 minutes

Ingredients:

1 ¾ cups white whole wheat flour

1 tsp. baking powder

½ tsp. baking soda

½ tsp. salt

2 eggs

½ cup melted butter or coconut oil

½ cup maple syrup

1 tsp. vanilla

Zest of one lemon

Juice of one lemon

1½ cups blueberries, fresh or frozen

Directions:

1. Preheat the oven to 350 degrees and grease a muffin pan.
2. Mix the dry ingredients together in a small bowl.
3. In a large bowl, mix together the eggs, melted butter or coconut oil, maple syrup, vanilla, lemon zest, and lemon juice. Add the dry ingredients and mix until combined.
4. Fold in the blueberries by pouring them into the batter and gently turning the batter over several times to mix in the berries. This is a gentler motion than stirring, which would spread the blueberry juice throughout the dough and turn it blue.
5. Bake for 15 to 20 minutes, or until a toothpick inserted in the center of a muffin comes out clean (no raw batter sticking to it). If you let the muffins bake too long, they'll be dry.

Cool the muffins on a wire rack, then store them in an airtight container. If you don't plan on eating them within a few days, freeze them.

These carrot muffins are a delicious snack that includes fruit and vegetables in every bite.

CARROT MUFFINS. These healthy, delicious carrot muffins smell amazing while they're baking. Their sweet cinnamon flavor is so good, and nobody will complain about eating their vegetables with this recipe.

Yield: 12 muffins
Serving Size: one muffin

Prep Time: 15 minutes
Cook Time: 20 minutes

Ingredients:
2 cups white whole wheat
    flour
1 tsp. baking powder

½ tsp. baking soda
½ tsp. salt
1 tsp. cinnamon

2 eggs

½ cup pure maple syrup

½ cup melted butter or
   coconut oil

½ cup applesauce

1 tsp. vanilla extract

1½ cups grated carrots
   (about 3 medium carrots)

Directions:

1. Preheat the oven to 350 degrees and grease a muffin pan.
2. In a medium bowl, mix together the dry ingredients and set aside.
3. In a large bowl, stir together the eggs, maple syrup, melted butter or coconut oil, applesauce, and vanilla extract. Add the dry ingredients and stir until just combined.
4. Stir in the carrots.
5. Transfer the batter to the muffin pan. Bake for 20 to 25 minutes, or until a toothpick inserted in the center of a muffin comes out clean.

Store these muffins in an airtight container at room temperature for up to 3 days, or freeze for several months.

BANANA BREAD. Brown bananas were made for banana bread. I get excited when I see overly ripe bananas in my fruit bowl, because this is one of my favorite snacks. It barely requires any additional sugar because the bananas are naturally sweet, and they bring a nice texture to this treat.

If you have a couple ripe bananas but no time to bake a loaf of bread, you can put them in the freezer right in their skin and save them for another day. When you're getting ready to bake banana bread, defrost the bananas and remove the fruit from the peel. You won't even have to mash them this way.

Yield: 9 by 5 inch loaf
Serving Size: 1 slice

Prep Time: 15 minutes
Cook Time: 40 minutes

Ingredients:

2 cups white whole wheat
   flour
¾ tsp. baking soda
¼ tsp. salt
3 medium ripe bananas,
   mashed

2 eggs
⅓ cup milk
¼ cup melted butter or
   coconut oil
¼ cup sugar

Directions:

1. Preheat the oven to 350 degrees and grease a 9 by 5 inch loaf pan with butter.
2. In a medium bowl, mix the dry ingredients.
3. In a large bowl, mix the mashed banana, eggs, milk, butter or coconut oil, and sugar.
4. Add the dry ingredients to the wet ingredients and stir to combine well.
5. Bake for 40 to 50 minutes, or until a toothpick inserted in the center comes out clean.
6. Cool on a wire rack.

Store this bread in an airtight container at room temperature for up to 3 days, or freeze for several months.

Variation:

My sister-in-law once told me that she likes to put nuts in her banana bread so she can call it "lunch." I like to put chocolate chips in my banana bread so I can call it "dessert," although I do like it with walnuts, too. You can add ¾ cup walnuts, chocolate chips, or blueberries to make this bread a little extra special. For chocolate banana bread, substitute ¼ cup cocoa powder for ¼ cup of the flour.

Tip

When you're baking with bananas, you want them to be very ripe. Ripe bananas have brown spots, and this is a sign the banana is nice and sweet. When bananas are still yellow with a bit of green, they aren't sweet enough for baking. If you're lucky enough to have too many brown bananas on your counter to use, freeze them for future baked goods or smoothies. You can slice the bananas before freezing to make them easier to handle for smoothies.

CRANBERRY ORANGE BREAD. I love to stock up on cranberries when they come to the market during the fall. I freeze several bags each year, and I can make this delicious bread whenever I want. Cranberries and orange are a delicious combination. This is a great fall treat, and you can even add it to your Thanksgiving table.

Yield: 9 by 5 inch loaf   *Prep Time: 20 minutes*
Serving Size: 1 slice   *Cook Time: 40 minutes*

Ingredients:
2 cups white whole wheat flour

⅓ cup melted butter or coconut oil

1 tsp. baking powder

1 egg

¼ tsp. baking soda

1 cup chopped cranberries

¾ tsp. salt

⅔ cup sugar

¾ cup orange juice

Directions:

1. Preheat the oven to 350 degrees and grease a 9 by 5 inch loaf pan.
2. In a small bowl, stir together the flour, baking powder, baking soda, and salt.
3. In a large bowl, mix the sugar, orange juice, melted butter or coconut oil, and egg. Add the dry ingredients to the wet ingredients and stir to combine evenly.
4. Coarsely chop the cranberries in a food processor or by hand. Fold the chopped cranberries into the batter. If you leave the cranberries whole, they'll be quite tart in the final product. Transfer the batter to the loaf pan.
5. Bake for 40 to 50 minutes, until a toothpick inserted in the center comes out clean.

Cool on a wire rack before cutting. Store this bread in an airtight container at room temperature for up to 3 days, or freeze for several months.

Better Store-Bought Snacks

Even with the best intentions, nobody can make all their snacks from scratch. Most store-bought snack options are unhealthy, but there are some good choices out there. The following list includes nutritious snack items you can buy at the store that require little to no prep. Keep these on hand for when the homemade snack supply runs dry.

- Whole grain pretzels
- Energy bars (no sugar added)
- Whole grain crackers
- Rice cakes (single ingredient: brown rice)
- Nuts
- Dried Fruit
- Fresh fruit
- Fresh coconut
- Fresh vegetable strips
- Cheese
- Plain, whole milk yogurt

By providing everyone in your family with nutritious snacks, you'll equip them with the fuel they need to face the challenges of each day. Snack time isn't a time for sugary treats without nutritional value. You can keep things interesting by making a variety of the productive snacks found in this chapter, and your family will appreciate that they taste delicious, too.

Chapter Six
Veggies Front and Center

"Eat your vegetables."

Mothers everywhere have been repeating this mantra for generations. Mom may have been wrong about a lot of things, but she was right about this one. I'm not a doctor or a nutritionist, but I know that eating lots of veggies is one of the best things you can do for your health. Vegetables are full of nutrients and fiber. Eating a diet with a generous variety of vegetables can minimize your risk of heart disease, stroke, cancer, diabetes, and obesity.

Given their well-documented health benefits, you'd think people would be lining up to stockpile vegetables. But no, human nature and taste buds have gotten in the way. Most of us would rather eat a brownie than a plate of broccoli, even though we know better. Many parents get discouraged when their children shun the vegetables on their dinner plates. They sometimes give up, saying their children are "picky eaters" who just won't eat their veggies.

I've always loved vegetables, but I do have days when I don't eat as much produce as I should. I occasionally find myself looking back on my day and wondering, "Do potato chips count?" There are always vegetables on my dinner plate, but I don't typically think of them at other times of day. This is where meal planning comes into play again. If you want to be sure that your family eats the recommended five or more servings of fruits and vegetables every day, you need to be intentional about plugging these foods into your meal plan.

Definition: Serving Size

We're supposed to eat at least five servings a day of fruits and vegetables, but how much is a serving size? According to the American Heart Association, there's one serving in one cup of raw leafy vegetables, a half cup of other vegetables, and a half cup of vegetable juice. One medium piece of fruit is a single serving, as well as a half cup of chopped, cooked, or canned fruit.

One of the best ways to ensure that you'll eat a wide variety of vegetables is to join a CSA farm share or a food co-op. As discussed in Chapter 3, these programs involve getting a weekly (or bi-monthly) share of local, seasonal produce. You don't choose what vegetables go into your box; you get what you get, with a little flexibility at some farms.

I used to have a fairly short list of vegetables that I would pick up at the grocery store each week. Then, after I joined a farm share, many new vegetables started to make an appearance in my kitchen. I don't know how I ever lived without my farm share. It's introduced me to so many new goodies that I had never tried before.

reen vegetables are among the healthiest foods out there, and there are so many different ways to enjoy them.

Green Goodness

Green vegetables are the crown jewel of the vegetable family. Full of vitamins, minerals, antioxidants, and fiber, they can help keep you healthy and protect you against heart disease and diabetes. Many green veggies also have high water contents, so they help you stay hydrated. Kale, collard greens, Swiss chard, and arugula may be an acquired taste for some people, but it's worth the effort of trying to acquire the taste.

When shopping for salad greens, choose anything but iceberg lettuce. This is the most frequently eaten green vegetable in the United States, and it's also the least nutritious. Iceberg lettuce isn't *bad* for you, but it contains little nutritional benefit because it's mostly made of water. Better choices include romaine, red leaf, and green leaf lettuce. In many cases, darker, more vibrant vegetables tend to have higher nutritional value.

To store leafy greens and fresh herbs, wash their full leaves in the bowl of a salad spinner. Keep washing until the dirt is gone, and dry them completely. Store each set of greens in its own airtight container with a paper towel on the bottom and the top of the pile of greens. With this method, lettuce should last for a week and herbs can last up to two weeks.

Tip

Many people are concerned about the health impact of pesticides on their food. Unfortunately, organic produce typically costs more than conventionally grown produce. If you'd like to buy some organic produce but can't afford to buy everything organic, check out Appendix 3 to see which types of produce have the highest and lowest amounts of pesticides.

SALAD. A salad is one of the easiest ways to get a bunch of veggies on your plate all at once. It doesn't require cooking, so it can be prepared quickly. There are so many different salad combinations, so it's a good idea to experiment. One of my children is happy to eat salad in many different forms, and the other child isn't as excited about it. But I've discovered that if I add grapes, dried cranberries, or berries to an otherwise veggie-filled salad, it gets a much warmer reception from the hesitant one.

To build a salad, I recommend including at least three different vegetables. Lettuce is the traditional base, but you can also make salad without lettuce. Nuts, seeds, cheese, or meat can be added to increase the flavor and protein. A bit of fruit will sweeten the final product, and many people enjoy the combination of sweet and savory flavors. Use the chart below for ideas of how to build a fabulous salad.

SALAD FIXINGS BAR
PREPARATION CHART

GREENS	OTHER VEGGIES	PROTEIN	FRUIT
Romaine	Carrots	Walnuts	Grapes
Green Leaf Lettuce	Green Peppers	Pecans	Berries
Red Leaf Lettuce	Red Peppers	Almonds	Mango
Arugula	Cucumbers	Sunflower Seeds	Pear
Spinach	Celery	Diced Cheese	Apple
Mustard Greens	Tomatoes	Diced Cooked Chicken	Raisins
Kale	Scallions	Diced Hard Boiled Egg	Dried Cranberries
	Radishes	Chopped Bacon	Avocado

> ## Warning
>
> Store-bought salad dressing is typically full of unhealthy preservatives. A simple homemade dressing of olive oil and vinegar, along with a sprinkle of salt and a bit of honey, is a delicious way to dress a salad. See page 216 for my homemade ranch dressing recipe.

LEAFY GREENS ON THEIR OWN. Leafy greens aren't just for salads. They can also stand on their own or play side dish to a main course. Kale, spinach, and Swiss chard are just a few of the powerhouse greens that can add color to your dinner plate and nutrients to your smoothie (p. 98). Leafy green vegetables can also be added to soups and stews for extra flavor and nutrition.

When shopping for greens, look for crisp, brightly colored leaves. If they look wilted or feel rubbery, they're past their prime. Fresh greens can be frozen if you're not ready to eat them right away. Before freezing, blanch the greens by boiling them for a minute and then submerging them in ice water to stop the cooking. This process will lock the nutrients into the greens before freezing.

Kale is a superstar in the leafy green vegetable family. It's an excellent source of vitamins A, C, and K, which are high antioxidant vitamins. It's also a good source of calcium and fiber. The most common varieties of kale are curly kale and dinosaur (or Lacinato) kale. You may find a recipe that calls for one or the other. Their appearance is slightly different, but they taste so similar that they can be used interchangeably.

KALE CHIPS. My favorite way to eat kale is in the form of kale chips. Honestly, I can eat an entire bunch of these. They taste similar to potato chips, which are one of my vices. If you have a dehydrator, follow the instructions to make kale chips in your machine. Otherwise, you can bake them in the oven as described below.

Yield: 1 bunch   *Prep Time: 5 minutes*
Serving Size: ¼ bunch   *Cook Time: 15 minutes*

Ingredients:
1 bunch of kale   1 tsp. salt
2 tbsp. olive oil

Directions:
1. Preheat the oven to 300 degrees.
2. Wash the kale and break it up into large pieces (3 or 4 inches).
3. Place the kale in a large bowl and add the olive oil. With your hands, mix it up so the oil is covering all the leaves. Sprinkle with the salt, and mix again with your hands.
4. Place the kale pieces in a single layer on 2 baking sheets. (If you only have enough kale to cover one baking sheet, cut the amount of oil and salt in half.)
5. Bake the kale for about 10 to 15 minutes, or a little longer if needed. Start checking on it at 5 minutes, and keep peeking in the oven every couple minutes after that. Once the kale starts to turn a darker shade of green, taste a piece and see if it's crunchy yet. If it's still chewy, let it keep cooking. Don't let the kale turn brown, though, or it will taste bitter. Some pieces will be done before others, so remove the pieces from the oven as they're done.
6. Serve immediately. These taste best the day they're made, but you can store the leftovers at room temperature in an airtight container. If they lose their crunch, put them under the broiler for a minute before serving.

Variation:
These kale chips are seasoned simply with salt, so they don't taste exactly like the highly seasoned kale chips you can buy at the store. Experiment with other spices, such as smoked paprika or cayenne pepper, if you want a stronger seasoning on your kale chips.

GREEN VEGETABLE SIDE DISHES. Broccoli, Brussels sprouts, asparagus, and green beans are delicious, healthy vegetables that go well as side dishes. When cooked properly, they add vibrant color to a meal. They also contribute fiber and nutrients that we all need. Kids may hesitate in the face of these "scary" vegetables, but it's important to keep offering them on their plates. It can take many exposures to a particular food before a child will start to like it.

If these vegetables are overcooked, they can lose some of their nutrient content and they don't taste very good. To properly steam broccoli and other firm green veggies, place the vegetables in a steaming basket in a pot with an inch of boiling water below. Steam them with the cover on the pot for just a couple minutes, until the vegetables are bright green and crisp-tender. If you cook them for an extra minute or two, the vegetables will become dark green and soggy.

Stir-frying these vegetables is another way to briefly cook them without overdoing it. The nutrients and flavor will stay intact if they're cooked just until they begin to get tender. In a hot wok, this only takes a couple minutes. Keep a careful eye on them, and pierce them with a fork to test for doneness.

Roasting and grilling green vegetables is also a good way to prepare them. This can bring out the natural sweetness in vegetables, so it may be a more appealing preparation for children. Again, you don't want to roast or grill them for so long that they get soggy. To grill smaller vegetables like green beans or Brussels sprouts, use a grilling basket so they don't fall through the grates.

Broccoli is one of the most nutritious cruciferous vegetables. It's high in fiber, antioxidants, and vitamins, and a serving of broccoli even provides some calcium to the mix. Most people just eat the dark green florets of broccoli, but the stem and leaves are full of nutrients, too. After you eat the florets, you can grate the stems and add them to soups or coleslaw.

BROCCOLI SALAD. Raw broccoli isn't always popular on veggie platters, but this recipe is a delicious way to enjoy raw broccoli. The dressing works so well with the salty and sweet add-ins. This salad is surprisingly addictive.

Yield: 4 cups   *Prep Time: 10 minutes*
Serving Size: 1 cup

Ingredients:

3½ cups chopped raw   2 tbsp. mayonnaise
   broccoli florets (1 sm. head)   2 tbsp. Greek yogurt
2 scallions (white & light   1 tbsp. honey
   green parts), diced   1 tbsp. white vinegar
¼ cup grapes cut in half or   4 slices bacon, crumbled
   raisins   (optional)
2 tbsp. diced walnuts

Directions:
1. Chop the broccoli into florets and dice the scallions.
2. Put the raw broccoli and scallions in a large bowl, and add the raisins or grapes and walnuts.
3. Stir the mayonnaise, yogurt, honey, and vinegar together in a small bowl and pour them over the broccoli mixture. Stir to combine. Sprinkle with the bacon if you're including it.
4. Refrigerate and serve cold or at room temperature.

Hot Potato

Potatoes get a bad rap. They're not bright and vibrant like many of the most nutritious vegetables, and some people think they taste a bit bland. But potatoes do have nutritional value, and they're one of the most versatile vegetables you can cook. A medium potato with its skin on contains nearly half the recommended daily allowance of vitamin C, as well as more potassium than a banana. With its neutral, adaptable flavor, a potato can fit in with just about any kind of meal.

Some produce does best stored in the refrigerator, while other items will last longer when stored at room temperature. Potatoes should be kept in a dark, dry area at room temperature. If potatoes are left out in the daylight, they may turn green and bitter. Refrigerated potatoes will become sweet and discolored. A small basket in a drawer or pantry is a great place to keep potatoes on hand. See Appendix 4 for a chart that will help you keep track of where to store various produce items.

Tip

If veggies like potatoes, carrots, onions, or celery are starting to look a little scary in your kitchen, put them in a container in the freezer with a label marked "veggies for broth." Then when you're ready to make vegetable broth or chicken broth, you'll have the perfect flavor enhancers ready to go. This is a good alternative to throwing them in the compost.

When shopping for potatoes, look for firm spuds without discoloration or bruises. There are many different variations, including russet, red, white, and fingerling. They can often be used interchangeably, although some recipes will call for a particular type.

Potatoes can last for weeks in a dark drawer, but after a while, they'll begin to grow little sprouts. These are harmless, but they should be trimmed off before cooking. Always scrub potatoes thoroughly before you cook them because you want to eat the skin. That's where lots of the potato's fiber and nutrients are stored

BAKED POTATOES. The easiest way to prepare a potato is to bake it. It takes about an hour in the oven, but you can forget about it while you're doing other things. Baked potatoes are forgiving, too. If you overcook them by a few minutes, it won't make a big difference.

Yield: 4 baked potatoes
Serving Size: 1 potato

Prep Time: 5 minutes
Cook Time: 60 minutes

Ingredients:
4 medium russet potatoes

Directions:
1. Preheat the oven to 400 degrees and scrub the potatoes. Pierce each potato a couple times with a fork.
2. Bake the potatoes on a baking sheet for 45 to 60 minutes, or until a sharp knife can be inserted easily into each potato. Baking times will vary according to the size of the potatoes.
3. Remove the potatoes from the oven and let them sit until they're cool enough to handle.
4. Cut in half and serve with any of the following toppings: butter, grated cheese, sour cream, chives, scallions, bacon bits, salt.

MASHED POTATOES. Mashed potatoes take a bit of work to make, but their unique, comforting flavor is worth the trouble. Russet potatoes make great mashed potatoes, but other varieties work too. If you're trying to add some extra vegetables to your family's diet, you can add some cauliflower purée to mashed potatoes.

Yield: 6 servings   *Prep Time: 15 minutes*
Serving Size: ⅔ cup   *Cook Time: 20 minutes*

Ingredients:

2 lb. russet potatoes, peeled if desired (about 4 medium)
¼ cup milk
3 tbsp. unsalted butter
½ tsp. salt (or to taste)

Directions:

1. Boil a large pot of water. Scrub the potatoes, cut them in half, and add them to the water.
2. Boil the potatoes for 15 to 25 minutes, or until quite tender. The cooking time will depend on the size of the potatoes. Pierce the potatoes with a fork to test if they're done, and remove each potato half from the boiling water with a slotted spoon once the fork goes in easily.
3. Let the potatoes cool for a couple minutes until you can handle them without burning yourself.
4. Mash the potatoes with a potato ricer, fork, stand mixer, hand mixer, or food processor.
5. Place the milk in a small saucepan. Heat the milk over medium until hot but not boiling, and melt the butter in it. Add this mixture to the mashed potatoes and mix well.
6. Stir in the salt, and then taste the mixture to see if it needs more salt. Adjust as needed.

Serve warm. Mashed potatoes taste best when they're made, but you can refrigerate or freeze the leftovers, too.

PAN-FRIED POTATOES. Pan-fried potatoes are a breakfast side dish staple, but I like to serve them at dinnertime, too. Also known as "home fries," they take a bit of time to cook on the stove. Luckily, it isn't hands-on time, so you can easily get these potatoes cooking on a back burner while you deal with the rest of the dinner prep.

Yield: 6 servings   *Prep Time: 10 minutes*
Serving size: 1 cup   *Cook Time: 30 minutes*

Ingredients:

1½ lb. potatoes, cut into bite-   1 to 1½ tsp. salt
   sized pieces   ½ tsp. smoked paprika
1 tbsp. olive oil or bacon fat   ¼ cup diced onion

Directions:
1. Scrub the potatoes thoroughly and chop them into bite-sized pieces. Leave the skins on the potatoes.
2. In a large covered skillet, cook the potatoes in the olive oil or bacon fat over medium-low heat for 5 minutes without stirring.
3. Stir the potatoes with a spatula. Add the seasonings and onion and stir again.
4. Continue to cook over medium-low heat for about 15 minutes, stirring every two minutes. If the onion bits are turning too brown, turn the heat down a bit. Keep the pan covered.
5. When the potatoes are tender, remove the cover and turn the heat up to medium. Cook for another minute or two to dry the potatoes out and brown them a bit. Serve warm.

BAKED SWEET POTATO FRIES. Sweet potatoes provide a slightly different nutrient profile than white potatoes, but both are valuable parts of a healthy diet. Rich in vitamins A and C, sweet potatoes are another versatile vegetable that can be prepared many different ways. My family loves this recipe for sweet potato fries.

Yield: 3 cups

Serving Size: 1/2 cup

Prep Time: 5 minutes

Cook Time: 20 minutes

Ingredients:

2 medium sweet potatoes
(about 1½ pounds)

2 tbsp. olive oil

1 tsp. salt

Directions:

1. Preheat the oven to 425 degrees.
2. Cut the sweet potatoes into strips (¼ inch – ½ inch thick).
3. Place the sweet potato strips in a bowl and add the olive oil. Stir gently so that all the strips are coated with oil.
4. Sprinkle salt evenly over the strips.
5. Arrange the strips on a baking sheet, making sure the thickest pieces are on the outside and the thinnest pieces are on the inside.
6. Bake for 7 minutes and then flip the fries. Continue baking for another 7to 10 minutes, until they're light brown and beginning to get crispy.
7. Cool slightly before serving.

Farmers' Market Finds

Farmers' markets have grown in popularity in recent years as consumer interest in buying directly from farmers has increased. With over 8,000 farmers' markets in the United States, many people have a great alternative to the grocery store produce that's flown in from other countries. By shopping at a farmers' market, you can support the local agricultural community and minimize your carbon footprint. You also reap the rewards of freshly picked produce, which is often much tastier and more nutritious than produce at the grocery store.

Travel Tip

When you travel on vacation, don't miss out on visiting the local farmers' market. This is a great way to discover local delicacies and support the economy at the same time. Many markets have live music, and they're often located near a playground or open space for the kids to explore. Visit at lunchtime for a unique, affordable meal for the family.

These markets can be expensive, though. When you shop there, it's a good idea to set a budget and bring cash with you. Make a shopping list, but also try a few new things. Focus on the fresh produce rather than the highly priced prepared goodies. At some farmers' markets, you'll want to get there early before the best items sell out. It doesn't hurt to show up at the end of the day either, though. Sometimes the vendors will lower their prices at day's end so they don't have to lug their produce back to the farm.

Farmers' markets are a good alternative to CSA farm shares for people who want to pick out exactly which vegetables they bring home. By depending on local farmers for your fruits and veggies, you'll be eating the freshest seasonal produce available. This will help you to maintain a varied diet over time, as one vegetable goes out of season when a new one reaches its peak. Once you've tried fresh tomatoes from the farmers' market, you'll never want to buy them at the grocery store again.

VINAIGRETTE COLESLAW. Cabbage is plentiful at the farmers' market, and it's the perfect base for coleslaw. I love having coleslaw on hand for an extra dose of veggies alongside my lunch or dinner. Its savory flavor combination is a great substitute for French fries or potato chips.

Whenever I make this recipe, I remember one of the biggest messes that ever hit my kitchen. I was in a hurry to put together a batch of slaw one afternoon before picking up my kids from school. I put the grated vegetables in a storage container and mixed together the dressing. After pouring the dressing over the vegetables, I put the top on the container and shook it up to mix everything together. I just missed one minor detail – the top wasn't all the way on the container. So as I shook the coleslaw, the top came off and the whole batch went flying all over the kitchen. Everything was covered with coleslaw, oil-based dressing and all. The moral of the story is this: if you use the "shake it up" mixing method, make sure the top is securely fastened before you shake away.

Yield: 7 cups   *Prep Time: 10 minutes*
Serving Size: 1 cup

Ingredients:
1 small head cabbage (red or   2 apples, grated
   green), thinly sliced   3 tbsp. rice vinegar
4 carrots, grated   2 tbsp. olive oil

1 tbsp. honey or maple syrup   Salt and pepper to taste

Directions:
1. Thinly slice the cabbage, and grate the carrots and apples. You can do this by hand or with a food processor.
2. Stir the cabbage, carrots, and apples together in a large bowl or storage container.
3. In a small bowl, stir together the rice vinegar, oil, honey or maple syrup, and salt. Pour most of the dressing over the cabbage mixture and stir to coat. Take a taste and add the rest of the dressing if needed.
4. Refrigerate for a few hours to let the flavors mingle.

Variations:
Coleslaw is nothing more than a cabbage-based salad, and there are so many different ways to make it. Add grated red, yellow, and green peppers for a rainbow slaw. For an Asian slaw, use Napa cabbage and add some fresh ginger. For a mayonnaise-based dressing, add a tablespoon of white vinegar and a tablespoon of honey to a third cup of mayonnaise.

Roasted cauliflower is an easy side dish full of nutrients.

ROASTED CAULIFLOWER. Cauliflower is another vegetable to look for at the farmers' market. In the same family as broccoli, cauliflower is one of my favorite fall side dishes. It's a good source of vitamin C, vitamin B-6, potassium, and fiber. Steaming and roasting cauliflower are two of the easiest ways to prepare it. If your head of cauliflower is bigger or smaller than the size in this recipe, adjust the amount of oil and salt accordingly.

Yield: 2½ cups
Serving Size: ½ cup

Prep Time: 5 minutes
Cook Time: 40 minutes

Ingredients:
4 cups cauliflower florets
   (from a 1¼ lb. head of
   cauliflower)

1 tbsp. olive oil
½ tsp. salt

Directions:

1. Preheat the oven to 375 degrees.
2. Remove the florets from the head of cauliflower and place them in a large roasting pan. Drizzle with the olive oil and mix it around with a large spoon (or your hands). Sprinkle with the salt.
3. Roast in the oven for 40 to 45 minutes, or until the cauliflower becomes tender and brown. Stir every 10 minutes.
4. Optional: When the cauliflower becomes tender and brown, turn on the broiler and place the cauliflower under it for a minute or two to dry it out. Keep a close eye on it so it doesn't burn.
5. Serve the cauliflower immediately, or store it in an airtight container in the refrigerator. If you're refrigerating it, put the cauliflower under the broiler for a minute or two to warm it up before serving.

ROASTED SPAGHETTI SQUASH. My farmers' market is overrun with squash in the fall. One of my favorite varieties is spaghetti squash. This is an excellent alternative to wheat pasta for those with gluten sensitivity. The strands of the cooked squash resemble spaghetti, and their mild flavor goes well with a variety of toppings. Spaghetti squash contains several essential vitamins and minerals. It's simple to roast in the oven.

Yield: 4 cups
Serving size: 1 cup

Prep Time: 15 minutes
Cook Time: 30 minutes

Ingredients:
2 lb. spaghetti squash
2 tsp. olive oil

¼ tsp. salt

Directions:

1. Preheat the oven to 400 degrees.
2. Cut the squash in half and remove the seeds and loose membrane from the middle of each half.
3. Coat the edge of each half with olive oil and place the halves cut side down on a cookie sheet.
4. Prick each section of squash 3 or 4 times with a fork.
5. Bake for 30 to 35 minutes, until the squash is tender when pierced with a sharp knife.
6. Remove from the oven, turn over the squash sections, and let them cool until you can comfortably handle them.
7. Scrape the strands of squash out of their shells with a fork. Top with marinara sauce (page 166) or another topping of your choice and serve warm.

Tip

Winter squash is a great vegetable to stock up on when you visit the farmers' market. Butternut, acorn, and delicata squash will keep at room temperature for many weeks, or even months. You can also freeze them for storage. To do this, first peel the squash and remove the seeds. Chop the squash into pieces and blanch them for a minute in boiling water. Then submerge the squash in ice water to stop the cooking, and freeze it in an airtight container.

FRESH-BASIL PESTO. Basil is an ingredient in so many classic summer dishes. From Caprese salad to fresh pesto, this is a wonderful herb that's plentiful at the farmers' market. Since I can't get enough pesto, I also grow it in pots scattered around my back yard in the summer.

Basil is a delicious garnish for pasta and other dishes, but the main reason I stock up on this herb is to make pesto. I make lots and lots of pesto throughout the summer, more than anyone could possibly eat. I freeze the excess in ice cube trays. These little cubes last me until February or March, and then I plant the seeds for the next spring.

Pesto is a flavorful spread for a sandwich, and I also love it as a pasta topping or calzone filling. This recipe is a good starting point, but I recommend you play with it to make it your own. I minimize the garlic in mine, but you may want to add more.

Yield: ½ cup   *Prep Time: 10 minutes*
Serving Size: 2 tablespoons

Ingredients:

3 cups basil leaves, lightly
   packed
1 small garlic clove, crushed
   (or to taste)

¼ cup olive oil
¼ cup walnuts or pine nuts
2 tbsp. grated parmesan
½ tsp. salt (or more to taste)

Directions:

1. Remove the basil leaves from the stems. Wash the leaves and dry them.
2. Crush the garlic clove with a garlic press, microplane, or mortar and pestle.
3. Place all the ingredients in a food processor and process until well-combined. You'll need to scrape down the sides a few times during processing.
4. Taste the pesto, and adjust the salt as needed. Since it's hard to get a precise measurement when measuring greens by the cup, you may need a couple extra tablespoons of olive oil if the pesto seems too dry.

This pesto can be stored in the refrigerator for several days. If you want to freeze some, place the pesto in an ice cube tray, filling each cube ¾ of the way. Cover with plastic wrap and freeze until solid. Then transfer the cubes to a zipper bag or other airtight container.

Soup's On

Soup is a great place to load up on veggies. When you have a vegetable that you're not sure what to do with or that seems like it's on its way out, throw it in a soup. There are so many different combinations that taste delicious.

When I make soup, I always try to make a big batch. It freezes well, and you can have it on hand for lunches and for those evenings when dinner preparations don't go according to plan. Glass containers are ideal for storing soup in the freezer. Make sure to leave at least an inch of empty space at the top of your container before freezing soup. Liquids expand when frozen, so if you fill a container all the way to the top with soup, it may break the container.

When making soup, it's important to soften the vegetables first before adding the broth. You may be tempted to skip this step if you're in a hurry, but don't. If the onions aren't properly softened, even an hour of simmering soup won't get rid of their crunch. I prefer chunky soups to puréed ones, so when recipes call for a full purée, I usually leave some texture in the final product. If you prefer puréed soups, you can adapt most chunky soup recipes by simply puréeing them to your liking. Experiment with recipes and make them your own.

A Dutch oven is a great pot for making a batch of soup. It heats evenly, and the vegetables and meat can be browned right in the pot before adding the broth. A large stainless steel soup pot works well, too. I also like the convenience of making soup in a slow cooker. You can put the ingredients together before you leave the house in the morning, and dinner will be ready when you get home.

Tip
The main challenge with slow cookers is that the heating temperatures vary from one model to the next. This is why many slow cooker recipes have a wide range of cooking times, such as "6 to 8 hours." My slow cooker runs hot, so recipes are usually done more quickly for me than what a recipe might suggest. Get to know your own slow cooker, and adjust cooking times as needed.

CARROT SOUP. A big bunch of carrots is a great farmers' market find. Carrots are a good source of several vitamins and minerals, as well as fiber. This carrot soup is a simple, comforting recipe that freezes well. Kids tend to like it because of its sweet flavor.

Yield: 7 cups   *Prep Time: 10 minutes*
Serving Size: one cup   *Cook Time: 45 minutes*

Ingredients:
1 tbsp. olive oil
¼ lb. chopped onion
2 lbs. peeled chopped carrots
½ lb. peeled chopped potato

6 cups chicken or vegetable broth
½ cup orange juice
1 tsp. salt (or to taste)

Directions:
1. In a large pot, sauté the onion in the olive oil until tender and translucent.
2. Add the carrots and potato and cook, covered, over medium-low heat until they soften.

3. Add the broth and orange juice, and season with salt. Start with one teaspoon of salt and add more at the end if needed.

4. Gently simmer for 30 to 40 minutes, until the vegetables are very tender. Purée with an immersion blender and serve warm.

Warning

When making soup, you need to be careful about how much salt you add. Some broths have a lot of salt in them, and some don't. I recommend waiting until the end to add the salt to soup. Taste it before adding any salt to see if it needs it. Then add a little at a time until you get it tasting the way you want it.

BUTTERNUT SQUASH APPLE SOUP. Here in New England, squash overruns the farmers' markets in the fall. It's not my favorite vegetable, but I've found several ways to enjoy it. This soup is one of them. Squash is rich in vitamin A, vitamin C, potassium, and fiber, and its bright color is a reminder that it's full of nutrients. The mix of squash, onions, and apples in this soup is a delicious combination of savory and sweet flavors.

Roasting the ingredients in this butternut squash apple soup brings out the delicious variety of flavors.

Yield: 4 cups

Serving Size: 1 cup

Prep Time: 20 minutes

Cook Time: 40 minutes

Ingredients:

1 ¼ lb. butternut squash, peeled and cut into 1-inch chunks (about 4 cups)

1 small onion, peeled and quartered

150

2 medium Granny Smith (or other) apples, peeled, cored, and quartered (cores removed)

1 tbsp. olive oil
½ tsp. salt
3 cups chicken or vegetable broth

Directions:
1. Preheat the oven to 375 degrees.
2. Place the squash, onions, and apples in a large roasting pan. Pour the olive oil over them and sprinkle with the salt.
3. Bake in the oven for about 40 minutes. Remove the pan from the oven every 10 minutes to stir the contents, then return it to the oven. Once everything is very tender when pierced with a fork, remove the pan to a cooling rack.
4. Warm the broth in a large pot. Add the cooked squash, onions, and apples. Purée the mixture with an immersion blender. Alternately, you can purée it in batches in a food processor or blender.
5. Serve warm and garnish with cream, diced scallions, and/or croutons.

Variation:
If you prefer a thicker soup, add an extra cup of butternut squash, or cut back on the amount of broth.

POTATO LEEK SOUP. Leeks and potatoes are readily available at farmers' markets, and their flavors are perfect together. This classic soup uses just four simple ingredients. It's a simple, comforting dish for a cool evening.

Yield: 8 cups
Serving Size: 1 cup

Prep Time: 10 minutes
Cook Time: 40 minutes

Ingredients:

1 tbsp. bacon fat, butter, or olive oil

3 large leeks, thinly sliced (white and light green parts only)

2½ lbs. potatoes, peeled and thinly sliced

5 cups broth

Directions

1. Melt the bacon fat in a large pot.
2. Place the leeks in the pot and sauté over medium heat for 5 minutes. If they start to turn brown, add a tablespoon of water.
3. Add the potatoes and broth. Bring to a boil, and then simmer for 30 minutes.
4. Purée the soup with an immersion blender or food processor. Taste it and add a little salt if needed.
5. Serve warm. You can garnish it with croutons, sliced leeks, bacon bits, scallions, chives, and/or other green herbs.

SLOW COOKER CORN CHOWDER. Fresh corn is one of the seasonal delights of summer. My family does get tired of eating corn on the cob, so this soup is usually the second thing I make when the corn starts pouring in from my farm share. Since nearly 90 percent of the corn grown in the United States is genetically modified, this is a great thing to buy at the farmers' market. You can ask the farmers directly if they use genetically modified seed to grow their corn. At the farmers' market, the answer is likely to be an indignant, "Of course not!"

Yield: 8 cups
Serving Size: 1 cup

Prep Time: 20 minutes
Cook Time: 6 to 8 hours

Ingredients:

6 slices of bacon
½ cup chopped onions
1 cup chopped carrots
2 lbs. red potatoes, peeled
and chopped

3 ears of corn, kernels
removed (about 2 ½ cups)
6 cups chicken broth
1 tsp. smoked paprika
Salt and pepper to taste

Directions:

1. Cook the 6 slices of bacon in the oven or in a frying pan. Pat the bacon dry, chop it into small pieces, and place it in a quart slow cooker.
2. Place all of the remaining ingredients in the slow cooker and stir.
3. Cook on low for 6 to 8 hours, or until the vegetables are all tender.
4. Purée the chowder with an immersion blender or food processor, leaving some chunks.
5. Season with additional salt and pepper if necessary, and garnish with cream if desired.

Including a wide variety of vegetables in your meal plan is one of the best things you can do for your family's health. Focus on local, seasonal produce to get the most bang for your veggie buck. Eating with the seasons is a great way to ensure variety, and it allows you to take advantage of the freshest available produce. Experiment with these recipes and make them your own. If you're lucky, you may find that you don't have to remind your kids to "eat their vegetables" anymore.

Chapter Seven
Dinner on the Table

If you're new to making home-cooked food, dinner is the best place to start. You can get more nutritional bang for your buck at dinnertime than almost any other meal. This tends to be the heftiest meal of the day, so you can make up for deficits from earlier in the day at the dinner table. Once you've broken the habit of hitting the takeout window several nights a week, it'll be easier to tackle the other meals of the day.

Dinner can be tricky to get on the table because it often comes at the end of a long workday. One of the things I enjoy least in life is actually *making* dinner at dinnertime. I'm hungry and cranky, and everyone around me is hungry and cranky. There's very little energy and patience to go around at dinnertime.

So I do whatever I can to get some of the dinner ready ahead of time. Whether I'm putting together a casserole the night before or chopping soup ingredients in the morning, I don't want to do *all* the dinner prep at 5:30. I'm usually okay to pull together the final details at that time, but I can't do everything.

Because of this, I'm a firm believer in the idea, "Cook once, eat twice." By making a double batch of a recipe, you can give yourself a break on another night. It doesn't take twice the time or effort to cook a double batch, so it's an efficient way to approach food preparation. Extras can be enjoyed for lunch, left in the refrigerator to eat for dinner later in the week, or frozen for another time.

If you have children, I recommend that you make a habit of preparing one dinner for the whole family. It may seem easier to appease everyone and make separate dinners for the adults and the kids, but this can cause more problems than it solves. Children need to be exposed to a wide variety of foods, and it often takes ten or more tries before they're comfortable with a given food. Instead of being a short order cook, you can make a "plain" version of many dishes and add extras like scallions or spices to the adults' plates.

Of course, there will be occasions when you want to make something for dinner that you know your children won't eat. As long as it's just once in a while, you can defrost something from the freezer that the kids will eat, then go ahead and try that exotic curry dish. I do suggest that you have the kids sample it, though. You never know.

Beans and Other Legumes

Beans are one of the most affordable protein sources available. Part of the legume family, beans are high in fiber as well as many essential nutrients. They're also rich in antioxidants, and they can help reduce the risk of diabetes and heart disease. Beans are a great staple to include regularly in your meal plans.

Beans are known as an "incomplete protein," which means that they don't contain all the essential amino acids that your body needs. You can combine beans with a second incomplete protein, such as rice, whole grain bread, or nuts, to get a complete protein. The second protein doesn't need to be included at the same meal as the first one; as long as they're eaten during the same day, you'll get the full dose of protein that your body needs.

Beans are one of the most affordable protein sources you'll find, and they can be used in so many different recipes.

Canned beans are convenient, but I usually use dried beans for several reasons. First, canned beans cost more than twice as much as homemade beans. The savings really do add up over time. Second, many canned beans contain unhealthy additives like calcium chloride and calcium disodium EDTA, which are added to help maintain the proper color and texture. And the third reason I cook my own beans is that I can eliminate the gassy side effects by cooking the beans with a small piece of kombu, a sea vegetable, in the cooking water. This may sound bizarre, but it makes a big difference in the digestibility of the beans. You can find kombu in the Asian section of many grocery stores.

Dried beans have a long shelf life, and they should be stored in airtight containers at room temperature out of direct light. It's best to cook beans within a year of purchasing them. If your beans have been sitting in the pantry for longer than a year, they may take longer than usual to soften, but they should still be okay to eat.

HOW TO COOK BEANS. It's very easy to cook your own beans. My family loves Mexican food, so I try to keep cooked beans on hand in my freezer at all times. Cooking beans take very little hands-on time, and there are just a few simple steps to remember. Most beans take between one and two hours to cook, although some may take longer. Be sure to check the package for the correct cooking time.

Yield: 5 to 6 cups   *Prep Time: 5 minutes*
Serving Size: ½ cup   *Cook Time: 2 hours*

Ingredients:
1 lb. dried beans (e.g. black, pinto, kidney beans, etc.)
1 inch by 2 inch piece of kombu

Directions:
1. Rinse the beans and pick out any debris. You'll occasionally come across a pebble or chunk of dirt.
2. Soak the beans overnight in water with a piece of kombu.
3. In the morning, remove the kombu and rinse the beans.

4. Return the beans and kombu to the pot. Fill the pot with fresh water at least an inch above the top of the beans.

5. Bring to a boil and simmer the beans over medium-low heat (covered) for 1 to 2 hours. Check the package directions for cooking times.

6. When the beans are tender but not yet falling apart, discard the kombu. Drain and rinse the beans.

7. Store the beans in the refrigerator for several days or in the freezer for several months.

Warning

Don't walk out of the kitchen when you're waiting for the beans to start boiling. I've made this mistake several times, and when I returned to the kitchen I had to deal with an overflowing mess. When a recipe calls for a simmer, always stay close to the pot while it's coming to a boil. Turn the heat down to medium-low as soon as it starts to boil. A simmer should just be a little sputter rather than a rolling boil.

Alternate Soaking Method: If you don't have enough time to soak the beans overnight, there's an alternate method. Boil a big pot of water on the stove and place the beans and the kombu in the boiling water for two minutes. Remove the pot from the stove and leave it covered for an hour to soak the beans.

VEGETARIAN CHILI. Chili is one of my favorite meals, and I rarely cook it the same way twice. Feel free to swap out different vegetables in this recipe while maintaining the bean/spice ratio. Adjust the seasonings according to your tastes, and add a diced jalapeno pepper if your family likes a little extra kick.

Yield: 8 cups   *Prep Time: 10 minutes*
Serving Size: 1 cup   *Cook Time: 40 minutes*

Ingredients:

1 tbsp. olive oil
1 small onion, chopped
2 stalks celery, chopped
1 bell pepper, chopped
28 oz. can diced tomatoes
4 cups cooked beans (any
   combination of pinto,
   black, or kidney beans, etc.)

2 cups fresh or frozen corn
   kernels
1 tbsp. chili powder
1 tsp. cumin
1 tsp. smoked paprika
1½ tsp. salt (or to taste)
1 cup broth

Directions:

1. Heat the oil in a large pot on medium and add the onion. Cover the pot and sauté the onion over medium-low heat for about 5 minutes (until soft).
2. Add the celery and bell pepper, then sauté in the covered pot for three more minutes. Add the chili powder, cumin, paprika, and salt. Stir to coat.
3. Add the tomatoes, beans, and corn. Stir and cook over medium heat for a few minutes.
4. Add the broth, cover the pot, and bring the chili just to a boil. Remove the top and lower the heat to medium-low. Simmer for at least 20 minutes. You can keep it on a low simmer for longer if you want the flavor to deepen, but

keep an eye on the chili to make sure you don't cook off too much liquid.

5. Serve with brown rice or cornbread. Top it off with any of the following: scallions, grated cheese, sour cream, tortilla chips, cilantro, lime juice, guacamole.

Variation:
To make meat chili, brown a pound of ground beef or turkey in the pot before proceeding with the above recipe. Remove the cooked meat from the pot and cook the onion as directed. Add the meat back to the pot with the tomatoes and continue as instructed.

TACO NIGHT. Taco Night is the perfect dinner for a family that has lots of different food preferences. Set up a taco bar with any of the following ingredients, and everyone can fill their own tacos with exactly what they like. The leftovers can be used to make a delicious taco salad the next day.

Tortillas. Flour tortillas, soft corn tortillas, and hard corn tortillas all work well for a taco bar. For corn tortillas, look for an organic brand with a short ingredient list if you want to avoid genetically modified corn. Most store-bought flour tortillas have long ingredient lists full of additives, but stores like Whole Foods Market do carry flour tortillas in the refrigerated section with short, clean ingredient lists.

Seasoning. Start with your own homemade taco seasoning (page 222). Store-bought seasonings tend to include ingredients like partially hydrogenated oils and maltodextrin, and they're also more expensive than homemade seasoning. You can make a big batch of taco seasoning and keep it in an airtight container with your spices.

Beans. I cook a one-pound package of black beans or pinto beans, which yields about 8 cups of cooked beans (p. 157). We eat half the beans at taco night, and I freeze the remaining half for next time. If your children don't like whole beans, mash them up for a refried bean consistency. You can stir in the taco seasoning after the beans are cooked.

Meat. Add a little cooked shredded chicken, ground turkey, or ground beef to your taco bar. This meat can also be flavored with taco seasoning. If you don't eat meat, you can skip it altogether and still have a hearty vegetarian meal.

Cheese. I include a little shredded cheddar or other cheese in my taco night spread. If you want the cheese to be melted, place the filled tacos in a 350 degree oven for about 5 minutes. Keep a close watch on them.

Veggies. I like a lot of veggies in my tacos, so I offer several vegetables. We typically enjoy lettuce, shredded carrots, peppers, and scallions in our tacos.

Salsa. My children don't always include salsa, but I think it's the best part of a taco. Homemade salsas are a great touch, but store-bought salsa works, too. Many jarred salsas contain added sugar and thickeners, but most stores carry a few versions of salsa with clean ingredient lists. Don't forget to read the labels.

You can store leftover taco fillings in airtight containers in the refrigerator. The leftover meat and beans can be frozen for another day, or everything can be tossed together in a big bowl for taco salad.

SLOW COOKER BLACK BEAN SOUP. At just $.40 per serving, this black bean soup is one of the most affordable dinners you can put on the table. This basic recipe can be adapted to suit your tastes. Increase the amount of seasoning or add a few of the optional "extras" listed at the end of the ingredient list. You can freeze the leftovers for a busy night.

Yield: 8 cups   *Prep Time: 10 minutes*
Serving Size: 1 cup   *Cook Time: 8 hours*

Ingredients:

3 cups dried black beans

4 cups broth

2 cups water

¼ cup chopped onion

¼ cup chopped sundried
   tomatoes

4 oz. diced green chilis

1 tsp. smoked paprika

¼ tsp. cayenne pepper

2 tsp. salt, or to taste

Garnish with grated cheese, salsa, cilantro, scallions, crushed tortilla chips, and/or avocado (optional)

Directions:

1. Soak the beans in a pot of water overnight. Drain and rinse the beans in the morning.
2. Transfer the beans to a slow cooker and add the remaining ingredients except the garnish ingredients.
3. Cook on low for 6-8 hours, or until the beans are very soft. Purée the soup a bit with an immersion blender.
4. Garnish with any of the suggested toppings.

LENTIL SWEET POTATO CASSEROLE. My husband and I love this Lentil Sweet Potato Casserole, adapted from *Vegetarian Times* magazine. This colorful combination of vegetables and lentils makes the perfect meal when we want to feel healthy again after we've been eating poorly for a few days. It's a great combination of spicy and sweet.

Yield: 6 cups
Serving Size: 1 cup

Prep Time: 10 minutes
Cook Time: 50 minutes

Ingredients:

1½ cups cooked lentils
2 cups chopped, peeled sweet potatoes
1 red pepper, chopped
1 cup fresh green beans, cut into one-inch pieces
½ cup raisins

2 tbsp. olive oil
1 cup broth
½ tbsp. diced ginger or ½ tsp. ground ginger
1 clove garlic, diced
½ tsp. curry powder

Directions:

1. Cook the lentils according to the package directions for a yield of 1½ cups cooked lentils.
2. Preheat the oven to 400 degrees.
3. Mix the cooked lentils, sweet potatoes, red pepper, green beans, and raisins in a large bowl.
4. In a medium bowl, mix the olive oil, broth, ginger, garlic, and curry powder. Pour evenly over the vegetable mixture.
5. Transfer the vegetable mixture to a covered casserole dish.
6. Bake, covered, for about 30 minutes, or until the vegetables are tender.
7. Serve warm over rice or on its own. If you don't want the broth in the final product, you can strain it out by

removing the lentil mixture from the casserole dish with a slotted spoon.

Quick and Easy Pasta

I have a complicated history with tomatoes. For the first 20 years of my life, I wouldn't go near a tomato or eat anything derived from tomatoes. I was "that kid" who refused to eat pizza, and I didn't want to be in the same room as ketchup or pasta sauce. Tomato juice sounded like a cruel joke, and fresh tomatoes were enough to kill an otherwise decent salad.

Fresh tomatoes are a delicious gift of summertime.

Then one day in college, I was at a gathering where pizza was being served. I decided it was time to get past this whole tomato thing. I tried a slice, and I can still remember how delicious that greasy piece of pizza tasted. I've embraced tomatoes ever since. But I didn't know until a few years ago just how delicious a tomato really can be.

Tomatoes fresh off the vine are amazing, and the grocery store version just doesn't compare. You need to find a source of fresh, local tomatoes to understand what I'm talking about. Whether you grow your own, buy them at the farmers' market, or sign up for a farm share, you're missing out on one of life's simple pleasures if you don't have a source of fresh summer tomatoes in your life. They bring pasta dishes to a whole new level.

As for the pasta itself, I recommend focusing on whole wheat pasta rather than white flour pasta. If the first ingredient listed on the package is "wheat flour" or "durum wheat flour," it's white flour pasta. The package needs to say "*whole* wheat" in order to be whole grain pasta.

The transition from white pasta to whole wheat pasta can be a challenge for some families. If your family can't handle whole wheat pasta at first, mix it in with some white pasta while everyone is getting used to the new texture. Over time, you can cut back on the amount of white pasta. Also, experiment with whole wheat spaghetti, short pasta, and lasagna noodles to see if one type goes over better than the others.

When cooking pasta, boil the water completely before adding the dried pasta. Stir every few minutes to ensure even cooking. Consult the package for the appropriate cooking time, and start checking for doneness a minute or two before the package instructions dictate. Pasta is best when it's cooked "al dente," which means it's tender but still firm. Overcooked pasta is mushy and falls apart easily. This detracts from the texture of the dish.

MARINARA SAUCE. When I get a big batch of tomatoes from my farm share, one of my favorite things to make is fresh marinara sauce. This recipe is easy to make, and the flavor is incredible. It can be served with pasta, on pizza, or as a dip. This marinara sauce freezes well, so you can stash some of it for a cold winter night.

Yield: 5 cups

Serving Size: ½ cup

Prep Time: 20 minutes

Cook Time: 2 hours

Ingredients:

2 tbsp. olive oil or bacon fat

2 small cloves garlic, minced

8 lbs. tomatoes

2 sprigs fresh basil

2 tbsp. honey

1 tsp. salt

¼ tsp. pepper

⅛ tsp. crushed red pepper, optional

Directions:

1. Fill a large pot with water and bring to a boil. Place the tomatoes in the boiling water for about 30 seconds, then transfer them to a large bowl of ice water. You may need to do this in two batches.

2. Remove the skin from the tomatoes. Cut off the cores and remove the seeds. You can do this by scraping the seeds out with your finger, and it's okay if you don't get them all. (I use food-prep gloves to protect my sensitive hands.)

3. In a large pot or Dutch oven, cook the garlic in the oil over low heat for a minute.

4. Add the remaining ingredients and simmer over medium-low heat for about 2 hours, or until it reaches the consistency you like. Leave the cover on the pot for the first hour, then remove it to help the sauce thicken. You can turn the heat up a bit if you need it to thicken faster.

5. Remove the basil stalks and leaves. If you want a smoother consistency, this sauce can be puréed with an immersion blender or food processor.

Variation:
To make a meat sauce, brown half a pound of ground beef or turkey in the skillet before proceeding with this recipe. Remove the meat from the skillet to cook the garlic, and then add the meat back into the skillet with the remaining ingredients.

> *I really enjoyed making this from scratch...it [gave me] a great sense of accomplishment."* ~ *Andrea*

BAKED PASTA CASSEROLE. This 5-ingredient baked pasta casserole is an easy knock-off lasagna recipe that just about everyone loves. If you're cooking dinner for a new mom and her young family, this is a good one to make since it can go into the freezer until she's ready for it. Double the recipe and keep a batch for yourself, too.

This is a basic recipe that can be embellished. Add ground beef, sausage, peppers, or other vegetables for an even heartier dish.

Yield: 9 by 13 inch casserole　*Prep Time: 20 minutes*
Serving size: 4 x 4 inch piece　*Cook Time: 35 minutes*

Ingredients:
12 ounces short whole grain pasta
1½ cups ricotta cheese
1 egg

3 cups pasta sauce (p. 166 for marinara)
¾ cup grated mozzarella cheese

Directions:
1. Preheat the oven to 375 degrees.
2. Boil the pasta according to the package directions for an al dente texture. The pasta should still be a bit firm. Drain and rinse with cold water.
3. While the pasta is cooking, stir together the ricotta and the egg in a large bowl.
4. Add the cooked pasta to the ricotta mixture and stir to coat evenly.
5. In a 9 by 13 inch casserole dish, spread half the tomato sauce along the bottom of the dish.
6. Add the pasta mixture to the dish.
7. Pour the remaining tomato sauce on top of the pasta, and sprinkle with the grated cheese.
8. Cover with foil and bake for 25 minutes. Remove the foil and bake for another 5 to 10 minutes, until the grated cheese is melted and a few pieces of pasta are beginning to get brown.
9. Serve immediately. The leftovers can be refrigerated or frozen. The bake time will be longer if you put it in the oven while it's frozen. Keep it covered for the first 45 minutes, then take the cover off and keep an eye on it.

Tip

Cooking all this homemade food may seem like it'll take too much time. Be creative and efficient with food preparation to keep up with it. Some people like to cook all their dinners for the week during several hours over the weekend. Then all that's needed during the week is a quick reheat in the oven. Having a well-stocked freezer is very helpful, especially on busy nights.

MACARONI AND CHEESE. Mac & cheese is a classic American comfort food, but far too many people have only tried the boxed, neon orange version. Real, homemade macaroni and cheese tastes so much better, and it's a lot healthier to eat. I recommend getting into the habit of making your own macaroni and cheese, and use the boxed stuff only on rare occasion. You may find that your family doesn't want the packaged version anymore after they taste the real thing.

Yield: 9 by 13 inch casserole
Serving Size: 4 x 3 inch piece

Prep Time: 15 minutes
Cook Time: 30 minutes

Ingredients:
- 16 ounces whole wheat macaroni or small pasta
- 2 tbsp. butter
- 2 tbsp. white whole wheat flour
- 2 cups whole milk
- 1½ cups grated cheddar cheese (or other cheese)
- ½ tsp. salt
- ½ cup grated Parmesan or Romano cheese

Directions:
1. Preheat the oven to 350 degrees and grease a 9 by 13 inch pan.
2. Boil the pasta according to the package instructions. Drain and set aside.
3. In a skillet, melt the butter and add the flour. Whisk together over medium heat for a few minutes.
4. Gradually add the milk to the butter and flour. Bring to a simmer and then whisk for about 5 minutes over medium heat, until it starts to thicken a bit.
5. Remove the pan from the stove and stir in the cheddar cheese and salt. Add the cooked pasta and stir to coat evenly.

6. Transfer the mixture to the 9 by 13 inch pan and sprinkle the grated Parmesan on top. Cover with foil and bake for 20 minutes. Remove the foil and bake for about 10 more minutes, until the top begins to brown.
7. Serve warm.

Variations:

You can add some vegetables to your macaroni and cheese for a one-dish dinner. Stir in two cups of peas or broccoli before baking. Another option is to add 1½ cups of pumpkin or squash purée. This will brighten up the color of the dish while also adding nutrients.

LEMON BROCCOLI PASTA. This Lemon Broccoli Pasta is a delicious, easy recipe to put on the table for dinner. If you walk through the door at 5:30, you can be eating this meal by 6:00. The flavorful lemon topping mixes well with the savory dried tomatoes and Parmesan. This dish is very flexible, so feel free to substitute or add other vegetables you have on hand.

Yield: 12 cups
Serving Size: 1½ cups

Prep Time: 10 minutes
Cook Time: 15 minutes

Ingredients:

1 lb. whole wheat pasta (about 8 cups cooked)
3 cups broccoli florets
3 tbsp. olive oil, divided
1 red bell pepper, chopped
½ cup sundried tomatoes, chopped

¼ cup lemon juice
1 tsp. lemon zest
1½ tbsp. maple syrup
¼ cup diced walnuts, pine nuts, or other nuts
⅓ cup grated Parmesan cheese

Directions:

1. Boil the pasta according to the package directions.
2. While the pasta is cooking, pour ¼ cup water into a large skillet. Add the broccoli to the skillet, cover it, and steam the broccoli over medium high heat for 1 minute. Remove the top and cook over medium heat for another minute to remove most of the water.
3. Add 2 tablespoons of olive oil and the red pepper to the skillet. Sauté the broccoli and red pepper, covered, over medium heat for 2 minutes.
4. Add the dried tomatoes, lemon juice, lemon zest, maple syrup, and last tablespoon of olive oil. Stir everything together and cook for another minute.
5. Drain the cooked pasta and add it to the skillet. Stir the mixture and heat it over medium-low for 30 seconds to combine the flavors.
6. Serve warm. Garnish with the nuts and grated Parmesan.

"The flavor combo in this was unexpected and lovely! And pasta topped with nuts was a great idea. I'm glad I tried it!" ~ Heather

Meat and Seafood on the Menu

Meat has been a regular feature on dinner plates around the world for centuries. Still, this is one of the more controversial food categories. Some people embrace a vegetarian lifestyle for health and moral reasons. Others profess that you can't eat a healthy diet without meat. There are studies supporting both perspectives, so it's a good idea to think carefully about this issue and evaluate your philosophy about meat.

My family does eat meat sometimes, but it's rarely the centerpiece of our meal. I tend to think of meat as a side dish or flavor enhancer rather than the main event. The traditional "meat and potatoes" dinner with a big piece of steak on the plate pushes other important foods into the background. By filling up on too much meat, people don't get enough of the nutrients they need from other foods, like vegetables and whole grains.

Benefits of Grass-Fed Meats

Grass-fed beef has less fat, more vitamin E, and more beta carotene than grain-fed meat. Cows that are raised on corn tend to get sick, so they're often given antibiotics to prevent infections. Grass-fed beef with the "American Grass-fed" or "Food Alliance Certified" seals has been put through a third-party verification process to confirm that the meat was raised without hormones, antibiotics, or confinement. Many farmers' markets and local farms sell grass-fed meat. It tends to be more expensive than conventionally raised meat, so you may want to eat less of it in order to help absorb the higher cost.

When shopping for meat, it's ideal to purchase humanely raised products. Organic chicken, pork, and beef are raised on certified organic pastures and they're exclusively fed organic feed. This feed doesn't contain any genetically modified ingredients or animal by-products. Organic meat comes from animals that aren't exposed to hormones or antibiotics, and these animals have year-round access to the outdoors. Non-organic meat often comes from animals that were fed GMO grains and lived in crowded, unsanitary, indoor environments. Think about whether these factors are important to you, and read labels carefully to make sure you're comfortable with the meat you're buying.

Seafood is one of the most valuable sources of omega-3 fatty acids, which are essential for heart health and brain development. It's also a good source of lean protein. Living near the coast here in Massachusetts, I can get fresh, local seafood at farmers' markets and through seafood shares. In other parts of the country, you can get high quality seafood at seafood markets or health food stores. Frozen fish can be a good option, because it's often frozen shortly after being caught.

WHOLE CHICKEN. Learning to cook a whole chicken is an important basic skill that all home cooks in meat-eating households should have. It's more economical to cook a whole chicken than to buy the parts packaged individually. A 5-pound chicken yields about 14 servings, so it can feed your family for multiple days.

My kids love to eat chicken quesadillas with the leftovers. I simply place grated cheese and shredded chicken between two tortillas and bake it until the cheese is melted. Homemade chicken broth is also a great byproduct of cooking a whole chicken. I like to have a stockpile of broth in the freezer to make soup.

There are many recipes out there for roasting chicken, and I recommend trying a variety of recipes. Some recipes call for different fresh herbs and vegetables placed in or around the chicken. Experiment with different flavors to see what your family likes best. The instructions below explain how to cook a chicken in a slow cooker and in an oven.

Yield: 3½ lbs. cooked chicken
Serving size: 4 ounces

Prep Time: 15 minutes
Cook Time: 1½ hrs (oven) or 4 hrs (slow cooker)

Ingredients:

5 lb. whole chicken

1 small onion, peeled and
  quartered

2 celery stalks, cut into 2-inch
  pieces

1 tbsp. smoked paprika

1/2 tsp. chili powder

1/2 tsp. cumin

1/2 tsp. garlic powder

1 tsp. salt

1/4 tsp. cayenne pepper

Slow Cooker Directions:

1. Place the quartered onion and the celery pieces in the slow cooker.

2. Stir together the paprika, chili powder, cumin, garlic powder, salt, and cayenne pepper in a small bowl.

3. Prepare the chicken by removing the giblets. Sprinkle the seasoning over the chicken and rub it in a bit.

4. Place the chicken in the slow cooker. No liquid is necessary because the chicken will release liquid as it's cooking, but some people like to add a little water to the slow cooker.

5. Cook on low for 3 to 5 hours, or until a meat thermometer inserted in the breast comes to 165 degrees (175 degrees in thigh). Cook times can vary widely from one slow cooker to another, so start checking the chicken after 3 hours.

6. When the chicken is done, remove it to a large cutting board. Ideally your board will have an indentation around the edges to catch the drips. Remove the skin and discard it. Remove the meat from the chicken, and return the carcass to the slow cooker to make broth. The cooking liquid and vegetable pieces can stay in the slow cooker (See page 175 for broth instructions.)

7. Serve warm, or store the chicken in the refrigerator in an airtight container for a few days. The cooked meat can also be frozen for several months.

Oven Directions:

1. Preheat the oven to 425 degrees.
2. Place the onion and celery in a large, covered Dutch oven.
3. Stir together the paprika, chili powder, cumin, garlic powder, salt, and cayenne pepper in a small bowl.
4. Prepare the chicken by removing the giblets from the cavity. Sprinkle the seasoning over the chicken and rub it in.
5. Place the chicken in the Dutch oven. Cook for 1 hour, then check the temperature of the breast and thigh. Once the center of the breast reaches 165 degrees, it's done. It probably won't be done yet at the 1 hour mark, so return it to the oven and check it every 10 minutes until it's done.
6. When the chicken is done, remove it to a large cutting board with an indentation around the edges to catch the drips. Remove the skin and discard it. Take the meat off the chicken, and place the carcass back in the Dutch oven to make chicken broth. You can leave the cooking liquid and vegetable pieces in the pot. (See below for instructions.)
7. Serve warm, or store the chicken in the refrigerator in an airtight container for a few days. The cooked meat can also be frozen for several months.

Warning

Eating undercooked meat can lead to illness. If you don't have a meat thermometer, there are other ways to find out if your chicken is done. One way is to cut into the chicken and look at the juices that it releases. When the juices run clear, the chicken is probably done. If you want to play it even safer, you can cut further into the chicken and look at the meat. If it's no longer pink, it's done.

HOMEMADE CHICKEN BROTH. Homemade chicken broth is a very nourishing resource to have in your freezer. It makes wonderful soups, and it costs a fraction of what you'd pay for packaged broth. You can also control the ingredient list by making your own broth.

1. After cooking a whole chicken, return the carcass to the slow cooker or Dutch oven to make broth. Add a few of the following vegetables to the pot: carrots, onions, celery stalks, potatoes (cut into large pieces). If you have any fresh herbs on hand, you can add a couple stalks to the pot as well.

2. Add water to fill the slow cooker or Dutch oven three-quarters of the way to the top. If you're using a slow cooker, cook the broth on low for about 8 hours, or overnight. If you're using a Dutch oven, simmer the broth on the stovetop for at least an hour. If you have time to let it simmer for two or three hours, that's even better.

3. Strain the broth through a fine mesh sieve and discard the carcass and vegetables. Store the broth in the refrigerator for a few days, or freeze it for several months. This broth can be used to make any of the soups in this chapter or Chapter 6. You can also use it when you're cooking rice, quinoa, or other grains to give them extra flavor.

BARBECUE CHICKEN WITH APPLES AND BACON. If you don't have the time to cook a whole chicken, this recipe is a quick, easy alternative. It has just a few simple ingredients, and it's so delicious. Homemade barbecue sauce is very easy to make (page 224), and I recommend it over the store-bought version if you want to avoid unnecessary additives.

Yield: 4 6 oz. chicken breasts
Serving size: 1 breast

Prep time: 15 minutes
Cook time: 30 to 50 minutes

Ingredients:

1½ lbs. chicken breast (about 4 breasts)

8 slices of bacon

1 cup barbecue sauce (p. 224)

2 cups diced apples, peeled or unpeeled (½ inch square)

Directions:

1. Preheat the oven to 350 degrees.
2. Place the bacon in a large pan or cookie sheet with sides. Bake for about 10 minutes, or until the bacon is cooked to a chewy consistency. You want to brown the bacon, but you don't want it crispy. Depending on what type of baking dish you use, it may take closer to 15 minutes.
3. Transfer bacon to a plate lined with a paper towel. Let it sit until it's cool enough to handle.
4. While the bacon is cooking, trim the visible fat off the chicken breasts and chop the apples.
5. Wrap each breast with 2 slices of the cooked bacon and place them in a Dutch oven or other oven-safe baking dish.
6. Pour the barbecue sauce over the chicken, and add the diced apples to the Dutch oven. The apples will soften better if you have them sitting in the barbecue sauce around the chicken rather than on top of the chicken.

7. Cover the Dutch oven, and bake in the oven until the chicken reaches an internal temperature of 165 degrees. This should take between 30 and 50 minutes, depending on the thickness of the chicken. Insert a meat thermometer into one of the chicken breasts, and start checking the temperature after 30 minutes.

Serve warm.

Variation:
This recipe can be prepared in the slow cooker as well. However, the chicken will come out dry if you leave it in too long. In my slow cooker, this recipe takes about 2 hours, but it can take up to 6 hours. Insert a meat thermometer into the chicken if you're using the slow cooker and keep an eye on the internal temperature until it reaches 165 degrees. Once you've made it a few times in your slow cooker, you can simply note the cook time and skip the thermometer.

SLOPPY JOES. I've overcome my childhood tomato aversion, but I still shudder at the thought of ketchup. Old habits die hard. If I see a recipe that includes ketchup, I turn the page immediately. This Sloppy Joe recipe uses a home-seasoned tomato sauce to flavor this delicious dish. Serve it on a roll or over a baked potato for a filling, family-friendly meal.

Yield: 4 cups   *Prep Time: 10 minutes*
Serving Size: ⅔ cup   *Cook Time: 20 minutes*

Ingredients:
1 tbsp. olive oil, coconut oil,   1 small bell pepper, chopped
   or bacon fat   1 lb. ground beef or turkey
1 onion, chopped   2 tbsp. maple syrup or honey

1 tsp. chili powder

½ tsp. smoked paprika

¼ tsp. cumin

dash of cayenne pepper

1 tbsp. red wine vinegar

1 tbsp. soy sauce

2 cups tomato sauce

Directions:

1. Pour the oil into a large cast-iron skillet and add the onion. Cover and cook over medium-low heat for about 5 minutes, until translucent. Add the bell pepper and cook for a few more minutes.
2. Remove the vegetables from the skillet. Cook the meat until it's brown and cooked through.
3. Return the vegetables to the pan with the meat. Add the remaining ingredients and stir to combine evenly.
4. Simmer uncovered for about 10 minutes, stirring occasionally.

Serve warm on biscuits, rolls, or baked potatoes.

MAPLE GINGER SALMON. I like to serve salmon for dinner regularly. Rich in omega-3 fatty acids as well as several vitamins and minerals, this high-protein fish is a healthy addition to any diet. This preparation couldn't be easier, and the flavor is delicious.

Yield: 1 lb. salmon

Serving Size: 4 ounces

Prep Time: 5 minutes (30 min. marinating)

Cook Time: 20 minutes

Ingredients:

1 lb. salmon fillet

½ cup maple syrup

1 tbsp. soy sauce

1 tsp. diced ginger

1 clove garlic, minced

Directions:

1. Place the salmon in a 9-inch baking dish.
2. Stir together the syrup and soy sauce, and stir in the ginger and garlic. Pour the marinade over the salmon. Cover with foil and put it in the refrigerator for 30 minutes, flipping the fish once while it marinates.
3. Preheat the oven to 350 degrees.
4. Bake for 15 to 20 minutes. The salmon is done when it's a uniform, light pink color. Serve warm.

Tuna Cornbread Casserole is a great dinner that depends on pantry staples.

TUNA CORNBREAD CASSEROLE. Sometimes you need to pull together a meal that comes from pantry staples, and this tuna cornbread casserole fits the bill. This is one of the first non-dessert recipes I learned how to make, and it came from a special college mentor named Kim. She was the director of the Chaplains' Office when I was an undergraduate at Holy Cross, and she was one of a kind. Kim had a way of making everyone feel special.

I went on an immersion trip to Mexico at the end of my senior year, and Kim led the trip. One evening, we were all sitting outside on the patio, enjoying the warm air and the sound of the crickets. Kim was talking about food, and she started describing this unique tuna recipe that she and her husband loved. It sounded so good, I made her stop so I could grab a piece of paper to write down the recipe. A few years ago, Kim passed away after a battle with cancer.

Her compassion, confidence, and engaging demeanor deeply impacted many people who knew her. I think of her whenever we enjoy this dish.

Yield: 8 servings   *Prep Time: 20 minutes*
Serving Size: 1¼ cups   *Cook Time: 50 minutes*

Ingredients for the Base:

1 tbsp. olive oil

1 medium onion, diced

1 clove garlic, crushed

1½ tbsp. chili powder

½ tsp. salt

½ tsp. basil

½ tsp. oregano

1 tsp. honey

28 oz. can crushed tomatoes

5 oz. can tuna

2 cups cooked kidney beans

1½ cups grated cheddar

Ingredients for the Cornbread Topping:

1¼ cups whole grain
   cornmeal

¾ cup white whole wheat
   flour

1½ tsp. baking powder

½ tsp. baking soda

½ tsp. salt

2 eggs

1½ cups milk

2 tbsp. honey

3 tbsp. melted butter

Directions:
1. Preheat the oven to 400 degrees.
2. In a large pan, sauté the onion in the olive oil over medium-low heat until translucent and tender (about 5 minutes).
3. Add the garlic, chili powder, salt, honey, basil, and oregano. Stir and cook for another minute.
4. Add the tomatoes, tuna, and kidney beans to the pan. Carefully stir the mixture and turn the heat to medium.

Bring it to a simmer, and then lower the heat to medium-low. Cover and simmer gently for 20 minutes.

5. While it's simmering, prepare the cornbread batter. Stir together the dry ingredients in a small bowl and set it aside. In a large bowl, mix the eggs, milk, honey, and melted butter. Add the dry ingredients to the wet ingredients and stir until just combined.

6. Transfer the tuna mixture to a 9 by 13 inch pan. Spread the cornbread batter on top of tuna mixture.

7. Bake for 30 minutes, or until the cornbread is beginning to brown. A toothpick inserted into the center of the cornbread should come out clean.

8. Let the casserole stand for 5 minutes, then invert it onto a large platter or cutting board. The cornbread will be at the bottom and the tuna mixture will be on top. Cover the tuna mixture with the grated cheese, and serve when the cheese is melted.

Tip

Instead of buying boxed cornbread mix, use the recipe above to make a batch of cornbread. Simply bake the cornbread batter in a greased 9 inch by 9 inch pan at 400 degrees for about 20 minutes, or until a toothpick inserted in the center comes out clean.

International Specialties

Many North Americans are plagued by diet-related illnesses. One in three adults in the United States is obese, which is a startling number compared to Japan's obesity rate of less than five percent. We can learn from our neighbors around the world about how to eat better. Many Asian and Mediterranean countries focus on healthy food in their typical cuisine, and their diet-related illness rates are much lower than in the U.S.

Chinese, Japanese, Korean, and Thai food have all made their way into restaurants around the world. The food habits differ from one Asian country to the next, but there are several overlapping elements that contribute to good health in these countries.

Their diet is primarily plant-based, with meat taking a back seat to whole grains (especially rice), produce, legumes, and nuts. Fish are a primary source of protein. Asians tend to eat sugary foods much less frequently than Americans. Green tea is consumed regularly, and this is a good source of antioxidants and phytonutrients.

The Mediterranean diet is also primarily plant-based, with a focus on whole grains, produce, nuts, and legumes. Olives are a staple of the Mediterranean diet. They provide a good supply of fiber, iron, vitamin E, and monounsaturated fats. This high-fiber diet results in a heart-healthy population that has more stable blood sugar levels than we tend to have here in America.

It's a good idea to include some recipes from these other parts of the world in your meal plans. Instead of focusing on chicken nuggets and grilled cheese for your children, try some of the recipes below with your family. The seasonings are mild, and even a picky eater may find a new favorite dinner here.

ASIAN NOODLE BOWL. When I visited my brother in Japan years ago, I was impressed by the Japanese version of "fast food." There were noodle shops all over the place, and this is where a lot of people would stop for a quick lunch. Customers sit at a counter and order a bowl of noodles and vegetables in broth. This delicious meal didn't take longer to serve than a burger and fries would.

During my visit, I noticed that just about every Japanese person I saw walking down the street in Tokyo was slender. Given their focus on lighter, plant-based fare, I wasn't surprised. This Asian Rice Noodle Bowl is my version of Japanese fast food, and you can substitute many different types of vegetables in this dish.

Yield: 6 cups   *Prep Time: 10 minutes*
Serving Size: 1½ cups   *Cook Time: 20 minutes*

Ingredients:

8 ounces soba or brown rice noodles

2 cups broth

½ cup frozen peas or snap peas in their pods

3 carrots

1 red pepper

2 scallions, white and green parts

2 tbsp. soy sauce (or less if your broth is salty)

2 eggs

2 tsp. sesame seeds

Directions:

1. Boil the rice noodles in water according to the package directions. Drain, discard the cooking water, and set the noodles aside.

2. While the noodles are cooking, bring the broth just to a boil in a large pot. While the broth is heating up, thinly slice the carrots, red pepper, and scallions. Add the sliced vegetables and the peas to the simmering broth. Cook for 2 minutes.

3. Add the cooked noodles and soy sauce.
4. Whisk the eggs in a small bowl until they're a uniform yellow color, then slowly pour them into the pot. Stir in the eggs and cook for about a minute, until the eggs are set. There will be little bits of scrambled eggs throughout the dish.
5. Sprinkle with sesame seeds and serve warm. You can strain out the broth with a slotted spoon if you don't want a soupy consistency, but my family enjoys it with the broth.

Variation:
For a stronger Asian flavor, add ginger and garlic to the mix along with the vegetables.

ASIAN CHICKEN SALAD. This Asian chicken salad is another way to enjoy a variety of vegetables. The delicious sesame lime dressing provides the perfect seasoning for this dish. Different vegetables can be substituted according to what you have on hand, and you can omit the chicken for a vegetarian version.

Yield: 9 cups
Serving Size: 1½ cups

Prep Time: 10 minutes
Marinating Time: 30 minutes

Ingredients:
6 cups thinly sliced Napa or Savoy cabbage
1 cucumber, quartered and thinly sliced
3 scallions, finely chopped
1 cup mandarin orange sections (fresh or canned)
1 cup shredded cooked chicken

3 tbsp. sesame oil
1 tbsp. lime juice
2 tbsp. orange juice
1 tbsp. honey
½ tsp. ground ginger
1/4 tsp. salt
1 tbsp. sesame seeds

Directions:

1. Place the cabbage, cucumber, scallions, mandarin oranges, and chicken in a large bowl.
2. In a small jar, combine the sesame oil, lime juice, orange juice, honey, ginger, and salt. Shake well to combine the flavors.
3. Pour the dressing over the salad*. Let it sit for about 30 minutes to let the flavors come together, and toss it a few times during the 30 minutes. Garnish with sesame seeds and serve. (*If you won't be eating all the salad in one sitting, refrigerate the leftovers and dressing separately. Dress 30 minutes before serving.)

MEDITERRANEAN QUINOA SALAD. This Mediterranean dish brings together the many flavors of a traditional Greek salad. Quinoa adds a whole grain protein to the dish, so it can be served on its own for a light lunch or dinner. This delicious salad will keep in the refrigerator for several days.

Yield: 6 cups   *Prep Time: 15 minutes*
Serving Size: 1 cup   *Cook Time: 15 minutes*

Ingredients for Salad:

4 cups cooked quinoa (8 ounces dry quinoa)

½ cup pitted Kalamata olives, chopped

1 small cucumber, chopped

1 red pepper, chopped

2 tbsp. red onion, diced

1 cup cherry tomatoes, sliced in half

Fresh basil leaves and feta cheese for garnish, opt.

Ingredients for Dressing:

3 tbsp. olive oil

1 tbsp. lemon juice

1 tbsp. red wine vinegar

¼ tsp. dried oregano

¼ tsp. onion powder

¼ tsp. salt

¼ tsp. pepper

Directions:

1. Rinse the quinoa and cook it according to the package directions.
2. In a large bowl, stir together the olives, cucumber, red pepper, onion, and cherry tomatoes. Add the cooked quinoa.
3. In a small bowl, stir together the dressing ingredients to combine well.
4. Pour the dressing over the quinoa salad and stir. Taste and adjust the seasonings as desired. Garnish the salad with chopped fresh basil and feta cheese.

Serve warm, or at room temperature.

By expanding the variety of your homemade dinners, you'll improve your family's health as well as their mealtime enjoyment. Try just one new dinner recipe each week, and over time you'll create a rich arsenal of meals. Dinnertime is much easier when you have lots of different options that you're comfortable making. Putting home-cooked meals on the dinner table most nights of the week may be one of the hardest parts of conquering your kitchen, but it's a satisfying skill to master.

Chapter Eight
The Best Part: Dessert

Food is meant to be savored and enjoyed. I don't think I ever would have bothered learning how to cook if it hadn't been for dessert. The return on investment that comes from pulling a fresh batch of chocolate chip cookies out of the oven is unparalleled. Dessert is the food that makes people smile, and it's a good thing.

In American culture, some people demonize dessert and feel guilty about eating it. But dessert isn't the enemy. Excess is the enemy. Eating a bowl of ice cream doesn't lead to obesity. It's when someone gets in the habit of eating a whole pint of ice cream several nights a week that trouble starts to creep in.

Store-bought desserts are typically overloaded with sugar and chemicals, and they have little nutritional value. By learning to make desserts at home, you can cut out some of the junk. You'll also have a greater appreciation of what you're eating.

I fully support eating a decadent dessert on occasion. By that I mean once or twice a week, not once or twice a day. In my family, we take our kids out for donuts after church a couple times a month. The ingredients in those donuts are terrible, and the amount of sugar is over the top. But they're kids, and I don't want them to become fixated on "healthy eating." We strive to find balance in our diets, with nutritious food playing the starring role and treats playing the minor side character.

In my house, there's a fine line between snack and dessert. We all love sweets, and I don't want to deprive anyone of the pleasure of eating tasty treats. That's why I'm constantly on the lookout for new healthy sweets to add to my recipe box. By replacing unhealthy packaged desserts with homemade goodies, my family doesn't feel like they're missing out. On the days when there's no dessert on the menu, we can appreciate the delicious goodness of fresh fruit.

Fruit Fiesta

Fruit-based desserts provide some nourishment while satisfying a sweet tooth. It's nice to be able to chip away at your daily fruit quota and eat dessert at the same time. Fruit provides fiber, antioxidants, and a variety of nutrients that your body needs to stay healthy. A diet rich in fruits can help stave off heart disease, cancer, diabetes, and high blood pressure.

When shopping for fresh fruit, look for unblemished fruit that's ripe or almost ripe. Locally produced, organic fruit is the best option when it's in season. We make a habit of going berry-picking and apple-picking several times a year. When fresh fruit isn't readily available, frozen fruit is also a great thing to keep on hand. Since it's typically frozen right after harvesting, frozen fruit can be even fresher than what you find on the grocery store shelves. I always keep frozen berries and mangoes in my freezer. They're perfect for baking and for smoothies.

Saving Money on Produce

Don't be afraid of the "Reduced Produce" section at your grocery store. Dinged-up apples and bananas are perfect for baking, and you can get them at a fraction of the cost of first-quality fruit. If you don't have time to bake with them right away, you can freeze them to use in the future.

Some fruits are better off stored at room temperature, while others do well with refrigeration. Apples can stay fresh for up to two weeks in the refrigerator, but they get mealy when left out at room temperature for over a week. Mangoes, watermelon, and peaches should be stored at room temperature until they're ripe enough to eat. Berries keep best in the refrigerator when they're stored unwashed in a single layer. Place a paper towel at the bottom of the storage container to keep them from molding prematurely. For more information about proper produce storage, see Appendix 4, page 233.

BLUEBERRY PEACH CRISP. This blueberry peach crisp is a delicious, healthy fruit dessert that takes advantage of fresh summer produce. It's inspired by a recipe in the *Moosewood Restaurant Cooking for Health* cookbook. The Moosewood series is a great collection of vegetarian cookbooks that I've been using for a long time. It's helped me to expand my collection of non-meat dishes. This crisp recipe is very flexible, and you can substitute other types of fruit according to what's in season.

Yield: 9 by 13 inch crisp *Prep Time: 20 minutes*
Serving Size: 3 x 3 inch piece *Cook Time: 50 minutes*

Filling Ingredients:

4 medium peaches, sliced (and peeled if desired)

4 cups blueberries, fresh or frozen

1 tsp. cinnamon

1 tbsp. white whole wheat flour

½ cup maple syrup

Topping Ingredients:

1 cup rolled oats

1 cup whole grain cornmeal

1 cup finely diced nuts

¼ cup shredded coconut

½ cup maple syrup

½ tsp. cinnamon

¼ tsp. salt

⅓ cup melted butter or coconut oil

Ingredients

1. Preheat the oven to 375 degrees.
2. Prepare the fruit and put it in a large bowl. Add the remaining filling ingredients and stir to coat.
3. Place the filling in a 9 by 13 inch pan and bake, uncovered, for 30 minutes.
4. Meanwhile, prepare the crisp topping by mixing together all the topping ingredients in the large bowl that has been vacated by the filling ingredients.
5. After the filling has been in the oven for 30 minutes, remove the pan from the oven. Cover the fruit evenly with the crisp topping and return the pan to the oven.
6. Bake for another 20 minutes, or until the topping begins to brown.
7. Cool on a wire rack. Serve plain, or add whipped cream or ice cream.

FRUIT SALAD. You can put any number of combinations together to make a great fruit salad. It's nice to have different textures, so try to mix hard fruits like apples, melons, and pineapple with softer fruits such as berries and oranges. I like to add a little orange juice to amp up the flavor and keep the apples from getting brown. Experiment with different flavors that your family likes together.

Yield: 9 cups
Serving Size: ¾ cup   *Prep Time: 10 minutes*

Ingredients:
½ fresh pineapple   ½ lb. strawberries
2 oranges   ¼ cup orange juice
2 apples

Directions:
1. Chop all the fruit into small, bite-sized pieces.
2. Add the orange juice and stir to coat.
3. Store the fruit salad in an airtight container in the refrigerator for up to 4 days.

Warning

If you're including bananas in your fruit salad, add them just before serving. They'll get brown and mushy if you leave them in the salad too long. If you won't be eating the whole fruit salad in one sitting, slice fresh banana into the salad each time you're serving it.

Apple pie is the all-American dessert. It takes a bit of effort to make, but it's well worth it.

APPLE PIE. Apple pie is the all-American dessert, and it's one thing I learned to make before I left home. My mom has a ceramic pie dish with the apple pie recipe printed right on it, and that's the recipe I learned. Whenever she'd make an apple pie, my mother would pierce the crust with a fork to make the letter A. It wasn't until I was a teenager that I learned the A was for apple, not Annemarie. Ah, the narcissism of childhood...

This is the most labor-intensive recipe in this book, but the payoff is worth it. I recommend making your own crust, because store-bought crust is often full of hydrogenated oil, preservatives, and even artificial food coloring.

Yield: 9-inch pie
Serving Size: ⅛ of pie

Prep Time: 30 minutes
Cook Time: 60 minutes

Ingredients for the Crust:

2 cups white whole wheat flour (or a combination of all-purpose and whole wheat flour)

1 tsp. salt

¾ cup cold unsalted butter, sliced

1 tbsp. maple syrup

⅓ cup cold water

Ingredients for the Filling:

8 medium apples, peeled, cored, and thinly sliced

¼ cup maple syrup

¾ tsp. cinnamon

¼ tsp. nutmeg

¼ tsp. ginger

2 tbsp. white whole wheat flour

Directions:

1. To make the crust, mix the flour and salt in a large bowl.
2. Pour the flour mixture into a food processor and add the cold butter. Process the mixture until you have a crumbly, course meal.
3. Add 1 tablespoon of syrup plus 4 tablespoons of cold water and process. The texture may still be crumbly. Keep adding water one teaspoon at a time until the dough comes together into a ball. Don't add so much water that the texture becomes sticky.
4. Carefully remove the dough from the food processor and divide it into two balls. Flatten the balls into discs and cover each disc with wax paper. Refrigerate for 30 minutes.
5. Preheat the oven to 425 degrees.
6. Place the sliced apples in a large bowl and pour the maple syrup over them. In a small bowl, stir together the cinnamon, nutmeg, ginger, and flour. Sprinkle this mixture over the apples and stir to coat evenly.

7. Roll out both pieces of dough on a floured work surface. I like to roll the dough into a large circle directly on the wax paper so it's easy to transfer it to the pie dish. Each crust should be about ¼ inch thick, and the bottom one needs to be a little bigger than the top one.

8. To assemble the pie, place one crust in a 9-inch pie dish. Gently press it into the dish so that the crust edge reaches at least as far as the edge of the pan. Then fill the dish with the apple mixture. The apples will shrink while baking, so you want to use enough apples to pile them about an inch above the top of the pie pan. Place the second crust on top of the pie and pierce it several times with a fork.

9. Trim the excess crust around the edges of the pan with a sharp knife. Press the crusts together around the edge of the dish with a fork or your fingers.

10. Place the pie in the middle of the oven on a baking sheet (this will catch the drips if you have any). Bake at 425 degrees for 20 minutes, then turn the heat down to 325 degrees and bake for 40 more minutes. Let the pie cool for at least 30 minutes before cutting. The filling will solidify more effectively if you let the pie cool completely before cutting.

Frozen Fun

Frozen treats are one of the most popular food items in my house during the summer. My kids love to take a break from the heat with a popsicle or a bowl of ice cream. Frozen desserts are refreshing and hydrating, which is extra important during the summer. They're also among the quickest, easiest desserts to make.

Most packaged popsicles and ice cream have pretty scary ingredient lists, including things like high fructose corn syrup, artificial food coloring and sweeteners, highly processed oils, and corn flour. These ingredient lists typically have close to 20 items in them. To make ice cream or popsicles, you really only need a handful of ingredients. If you invest in a set of popsicle molds, an ice cream maker, or a snow cone machine, you'll save money in the long run and provide your family with healthier summertime desserts.

PUMPKIN ICE CREAM. I make lots of homemade ice cream during the warm months with my KitchenAid ice cream attachment. Free-standing ice cream makers work well too. This recipe for pumpkin ice cream is simple and rich. If you're dealing with a dairy allergy in your family, you can substitute full-fat coconut milk for a tasty alternative.

Yield: 12 scoops
Serving size: 2 scoops

Prep/Churn time: 25 minutes
Freeze time: 3 hours

Ingredients:

1 cup pumpkin purée
½ tsp. ground cinnamon
¼ tsp. ground ginger
⅛ tsp. ground nutmeg

1 cup heavy cream
½ cup whole milk
⅔ cup maple syrup or sugar
1 tsp. vanilla extract

Directions:
1. Combine the pumpkin purée, cinnamon, ginger, and nutmeg in a mixing bowl.
2. Add the remaining ingredients and mix until well combined.
3. Churn the mixture for 15 to 20 minutes according to your ice cream maker's instructions.

4. Transfer the mixture to a wide, shallow airtight container and place it in the freezer. It will reach an ideal scooping texture after about 3 hours.

5. Homemade ice cream tastes best the day it's made, but it can be stored for several days in the freezer. Once it's past its prime, you can fold the extra ice cream into a smoothie.

Tip

Homemade ice cream tends to solidify in the freezer more than store-bought ice cream, which contains chemicals to keep it softer. To easily scoop homemade ice cream, place it in the refrigerator for 20 minutes or on the counter for 10 minutes before scooping. Run your ice cream scooper under hot water to make scooping easier.

You can avoid the laundry list of preservatives found in commercially-made popsicles by making these simple fudge pops at home.

FUDGE POPSICLES. Creamy fudge popsicles were one of my favorite desserts as a child. Unfortunately, they contain 17 ingredients, including high fructose corn syrup, polysorbate 80, and carrageenan. These homemade banana fudge pops are a much better option. Sweet, creamy, and full of chocolate goodness, they take just minutes to make and you can enjoy them as soon as they're frozen. Kids won't realize they're eating a nutritious snack, and you won't have to worry about chemicals in their summer treats.

Yield: 4 popsicles
Serving size: 1 popsicle
  (½ cup)

Prep time: 5 minutes
Freeze time: 3 hours

Ingredients:

2 cups sliced ripe bananas
  (approximately 2 large
  bananas)
¼ cup cocoa powder

½ cup milk
2 tbsp. maple syrup
½ tsp. vanilla extract

Directions:

1. Place all the ingredients in a food processor or blender and process until smooth.
2. Transfer the mixture to popsicle molds and freeze.
3. To remove the popsicles from their molds, leave them out on the counter for a few minutes or run them under lukewarm water to loosen.

Artificial Food Colorings

Many types of artificial food coloring have been approved for use in America by the FDA. However, other countries around the world have banned or limited the use of artificial food coloring in packaged food. These chemicals are derived from petroleum, and studies have indicated that artificial food coloring may contribute to hyperactivity and cancer. If you buy popsicles or other brightly colored desserts at the grocery store, check the ingredient lists and choose products that use natural color enhancers instead of artificial dyes. Better yet, make your own.

CHOCOLATE NUT BARK FREEZER CANDY. This is one of my favorite healthy desserts. We have several chocoholics in our house, so I need to have nutritious chocolate recipes in my arsenal. This high-protein freezer candy fits the bill, and my daughter and husband can't get enough of it. Try this the next time you're craving chocolate. Your family will love you for it.

Yield: 24 pieces   *Prep time: 10 minutes*
Serving size: 2 x 2 inch piece   *Freeze time: 30 minutes*

Ingredients:

¼ cup chopped walnuts or cashews

¾ cup unsweetened shredded coconut

⅓ cup cocoa powder

¼ tsp. salt

¾ cup chunky peanut butter or other nut butter

¼ cup melted coconut oil

¼ cup maple syrup or honey

2 tsp. vanilla extract

Directions:
1. Mix together all the ingredients in a large mixing bowl.
2. Place a piece of wax paper on a cookie sheet, and spread the mixture out to a thickness of ¼ to ⅓ inch. I use my fingers to spread it out. It's a sticky mess at this point, but it will be worth it.
3. Place it in the freezer, uncovered, for 30 minutes.
4. After 30 minutes, cut the bark into pieces. Serve immediately or put it in an airtight container in the freezer until ready to serve. Don't leave the chocolate nut bark sitting out at room temperature or it will melt.

Fresh From the Oven

Classic baked desserts are the ultimate comfort food. Baking is a favorite pastime of many home cooks, probably because the payoff is so fabulous. I love having home-baked muffins and granola bars for snacks, but there's nothing like a decadent homemade dessert to get everyone smiling.

Baking is more of a science than other types of cooking. Flour, eggs, and baking soda have a significant impact on the structure of your baked goodies, so careful measurements are important. Home cooks need to get to know their ovens. Some ovens run hotter than others, so things can finish baking more quickly than a recipe would suggest. I always start checking my baked goods a few minutes before the recipe recommends. You can put something back in the oven to bake a little longer, but you can't reverse it once something is overcooked.

Many recipes for baked goods will tell you to let things cool before cutting or serving. I know it's hard to restrain yourself when you have a delicious treat fresh from the oven sitting on your counter, but letting an apple pie sit before cutting it is crucial if you don't want to have a runny mess on your hands. Homemade granola bars will fall apart if you cut them before they're cool, and a hot chocolate chip cookie could burn your tongue. Always follow the post-baking recipe instructions for the best results.

CHOCOLATE CHIP COOKIES. Chocolate chip cookies are the first dessert I mastered. I owned that recipe on the chocolate chip package. I made them so many times that I had memorized the recipe, and I looked for excuses to make them.

These days, I only make chocolate chip cookies once in a while, and I've swapped out some of the unhealthy elements. By adding more vanilla extract, I can cut back on the sugar without sacrificing flavor. And whole wheat or gluten-free flour taste just as good in this recipe as white flour. This is a rare use of white sugar in my kitchen, but I do use organic sugar because it's less refined than traditional white sugar.

Yield: 24 cookies

Serving Size: 2 cookies

Prep Time: 10 minutes

Cook Time: 20 minutes

Ingredients:

1 cup white whole wheat flour

½ tsp. baking soda

½ tsp. salt

1 stick butter, softened

⅔ cup white sugar (preferably organic)

1 egg

1 tsp. vanilla extract

1 cup chocolate chips

Directions:

1. Slice the butter into 10 pieces and let it sit at room temperature for about an hour to soften. If it's warm in your kitchen, you won't need as much time to let it soften.
2. Preheat the oven to 375 degrees.
3. In a small bowl, whisk together the flour, baking soda, and salt. Set aside.
4. In the bowl of a stand mixer, mix the butter and sugar for about 30 seconds, until uniform and fluffy. Add the egg and vanilla, and mix until combined.
5. Add the dry ingredients to the mixing bowl in 2 batches, and mix well after each addition to fully incorporate the flour. You'll need to scrape down the sides a couple times.
6. Stir in the chocolate chips.
7. Place heaping tablespoons of the dough on a cookie sheet. Make 3 rows of 3 cookies each. If you want them to be extra pretty, you can roll each tablespoon of dough into a

ball with your hands and then press it down slightly on the cookie sheet.

8. Bake the cookies on the center rack of the oven for 8 to 9 minutes. To save time, you can bake 2 trays at once on two racks in the oven, but they won't come out as uniformly.

9. Let the cookies cool for 2 minutes, then remove them with a spatula and place them on a wire rack to cool.

Measuring Ingredients

In baking recipes, it's a good idea to get fairly precise measurements of the dry ingredients. These ingredients shouldn't be packed down in the measuring cup. When measuring flour, loosely over-fill the measuring cup and then scrape the flat, non-sharp edge of a knife along the measuring cup to push off the excess flour. This will give you a nice, even surface of flour, ensuring that you have the correct amount. Use the same trick with measuring spoons to make sure your teaspoon of baking soda is really a teaspoon.

BROWNIES. There are a million brownie recipes out there, and I've made my fair share of them. From rich and fudgy to sweet and cake-like, I love them all. I actually have 3 different versions that I make depending on my mood. This is my "healthier" brownie recipe. It works as a snack or a dessert. Sweetened by dates, bananas, and maple syrup, it has a little less added sugar than your typical brownie without sacrificing flavor. You can use whole wheat flour or gluten-free flour with equal success here.

Yield: 9 by 13 inch pan
Serving Size: 3 x 3 inch piece

Prep Time: 20 minutes
Cook Time: 25 minutes

Ingredients:

1¼ cups white whole wheat flour

⅓ cup cocoa powder

½ tsp. salt

6 ounces unsweetened or semi-sweet chocolate

¾ cup melted butter or coconut oil

⅓ cup pitted, chopped Medjool dates (about 3)

½ ripe banana

1¼ cups pure maple syrup

4 eggs

1 tsp. vanilla extract

Directions:

1. Preheat the oven to 350 degrees and grease a 9 by 13 inch baking dish.
2. In a small bowl, combine the flour, cocoa powder, and salt. Set aside.
3. Melt the chocolate and the coconut oil in a small saucepan. Cool slightly.
4. Boil 2 cups of water in a small saucepan. Simmer the dates for 3 minutes to soften them.
5. In a food processor or blender, purée the dates, the banana, and 2 tablespoons of the date cooking water until smooth.
6. In a large bowl, combine the maple syrup, eggs, and vanilla. Add the dates, bananas, melted chocolate, and coconut oil. Stir to combine well.
7. Add the dry ingredients to the wet ingredients and mix well. Transfer the batter to the baking pan.
8. Bake for 20 to 25 minutes, or until they're set and a toothpick inserted in the center comes out with little bits of brownie stuck to it. In this recipe, if you wait until the toothpick comes out clean, the brownies may be dry.

Butter Substitutes

Many baking recipes call for butter. If you have a dairy allergy or sensitivity in your family, coconut oil is a great alternative and it can be substituted one to one. Alternately, if a recipe calls for coconut oil, melted butter will usually work in its place. It's difficult to soften coconut oil the way butter can be softened, but you can use melted coconut oil in place of softened or melted butter. The texture may be a bit different in your final product, but it will still be good.

COCONUT CHOCOLATE CHIP BARS. These bars are the perfect combination of chocolate and coconut in my book. They make a delicious treat that also happens to be pretty healthy. Coconut is rich in fiber, vitamins, and minerals, and these bars include both coconut oil and coconut meat. These delicate, cake-like bars are one of my favorite "just sweet enough" desserts.

Yield: 9 by 13 inch pan
Serving Size: 1 bar

Prep Time: 10 minutes
Cook Time: 30 minutes

Ingredients:
3 eggs
¼ cup melted coconut oil
1 cup whole milk or full-fat coconut milk
½ cup pure maple syrup
1 tsp. vanilla extract

1 cup white whole wheat flour
2 cups unsweetened shredded coconut
1 cup chocolate chips

Directions:

1. Preheat the oven to 350 degrees.
2. Mix together the eggs, coconut oil, milk, vanilla, and maple syrup in a large bowl.
3. Add the flour and coconut to the wet ingredients and mix to combine. Stir in the chocolate chips.
4. Pour the mixture into a 9 by 13 inch glass baking dish. Bake for 25 to 30 minutes, until it's set and the edges begin to turn light brown.
5. Cool completely on a wire rack. Cut into 16 bars.

PUMPKIN CAKE. I've been perfecting this pumpkin cake recipe for years. It's one of my favorite treats in the fall, and I can feel good about eating it and serving it to my family. Pumpkin recipes don't need as much oil or added moisture as other baked goods because the **puréed** pumpkin is so moist. This recipe uses white whole wheat flour, but it also works well with gluten-free flour.

Yield: 9 by 13 inch cake   *Prep Time: 10 minutes*
Serving Size: 3 x 3 inch piece   *Cook Time: 40 minutes*

Ingredients:

1¾ cups white whole wheat flour

2 tsp. baking soda

1 tsp. cinnamon

1 tsp. salt

4 eggs

¼ cup melted butter or coconut oil

⅔ cup maple syrup

⅓ cup applesauce

2 cups pumpkin purée

Directions:

1. Preheat the oven to 350 degrees and grease a 9 by 13 inch baking dish.
2. In a medium bowl, combine the flour, baking soda, cinnamon, and salt.
3. In a large bowl, combine the remaining ingredients.
4. Add the dry ingredients to the wet ingredients and stir until well combined.
5. Bake for 35 to 40 minutes, until the cake is set and a toothpick inserted in the center comes out clean.

Once you've mastered the art of making homemade desserts, you'll be less tempted to buy the boxed version. Your family is much better off without all the chemicals and food coloring found in store-bought desserts, and homemade goodies taste better, too. From fruity dishes to frozen treats to home-baked delicacies, these recipes will help you to control the sweet situation in your kitchen.

Chapter Nine
DIY Staples

It's empowering to learn how to cook your own food. This skill puts you in charge of what you eat. We all buy processed food and pick up takeout on occasion, but it's nice to know that we're choosing that route rather than being confined to it. When people don't know how to cook, that might be the only route they've ever considered.

In order to conquer your kitchen, you don't need to make all your food from scratch. But it's nice to know that you *could* make all your food from scratch. Nothing is out of reach. "I can't cook" becomes more of a scheduling issue than a matter of ability.

In this chapter, we'll look at different staples that many people tend to buy pre-made. Each recipe is simple and takes no longer than 10 minutes of hands-on time. These are building blocks to other recipes, and mastering them will help make the homemade food process easier for you.

By making homemade staples, you can save a lot of money. More importantly, you can control the ingredients that your family is eating. The store-bought versions of these items contain unnecessary additives that are best avoided. Whipped cream doesn't only come in a can, and taco seasoning doesn't have to come in a packet. You'll be amazed by the number of things you can make in your own kitchen.

Homemade Dairy Products

Many dairy products provide a generous supply of calcium, which is important for strong bones. Protein and vital nutrients are found in dairy products, too. Regular dairy intake is associated with maintaining healthy weight and blood pressure. Despite these benefits, a dairy-filled diet isn't healthy for everyone. Lactose intolerance and casein allergies are common, and many people have a difficult time digesting dairy. This isn't all that surprising, since cow's milk was made for cows. They have large stomachs with four compartments to manage the complex digestion process that goes along with dairy.

I have a dairy sensitivity, so I limit the amount of dairy products in my diet. I do like to have an occasional yogurt smoothie, and it would be challenging for me to live without cheese altogether. I look for high-quality cheese for the occasional indulgence, and I really do appreciate and savor it. I like to provide my family with high-quality dairy products, and several kinds can easily be made at home.

As with most processed foods, pre-packaged dairy products tend to include unnecessary preservatives, thickeners, and flavor-enhancers. You can make whipped cream, cheese, and yogurt without much effort at all. This section includes just a few examples of simple homemade dairy products.

Homemade whipped cream is a delicacy that couldn't be easier to make.

WHIPPED CREAM. I have fond memories of eating whipped cream out of the aerosol can as a child. When I look at the ingredient list on that can now, I shudder a bit. Canned whipped cream often has at least ten ingredients, including corn syrup and preservatives. All you need to make whipped cream is cream, and a little extra sweetener is nice too. I make it in a stand mixer, but my husband likes to whip cream by hand with a whisk. If you want an arm workout, feel free to do it his way.

Yield: 3 cups   *Prep Time: 5 minutes*

Ingredients:

1 cup heavy cream
2 tbsp. sugar or maple syrup
   (or to taste)

½ tsp. vanilla extract,
   optional

Directions:
1. Pour the ingredients in the bowl of a stand mixer.
2. Whip on medium speed for about 3 minutes, or until stiff peaks form. This means that when you lift the mixing whisk, a peak of whipped cream stands upright and doesn't fall back into the rest of the cream. Start checking after the first minute of mixing.
3. Serve immediately, or transfer to an airtight container in the refrigerator.

RICOTTA. Homemade ricotta couldn't be easier to make. You simply heat some milk on the stove and add lemon juice. It costs less than half the price of store-bought ricotta, so it's worth learning how to make it. You can use ricotta as a spread for crackers, a topping for pizza, a filling for lasagna, or a base for fluffy pancakes and cookies. My Baked Pasta Casserole on p. 167 features this delicious homemade ricotta.

Yield: 1½ cups   *Prep Time: 10 minutes*
                                   Strain Time: 1 hour

Ingredients:

4 cups milk

½ tsp. salt

2 tbsp. freshly squeezed
lemon juice

Directions:

1. In a medium heavy-bottomed pot, heat the milk on the stove over medium-low heat. Using a thermometer, raise the milk's temperature to 180 degrees.
2. Add the lemon juice and salt to the milk, and stir briefly to combine. Heat over a medium flame for another minute until it reaches 200 degrees.
3. Remove the pot from the stove and let it sit on the counter for 10 minutes. The cheese will form as the curds separate from the liquid. If you don't see thick cheese forming in the first minute, add a little more lemon juice.
4. After 10 minutes, transfer the mixture to a fine mesh strainer lined with butter muslin or cheesecloth.
5. Let the liquid drain thoroughly for an hour in the refrigerator. Transfer the cheese to an airtight container and store it for up to 5 days. The liquid can be used in place of buttermilk in another recipe.

Variation:

If you don't have lemon juice available, you can use plain white vinegar as the acid in this recipe.

Other Homemade Cheeses

Many other cheeses can be made at home. Mascarpone is one of the easiest, and the process is similar to homemade ricotta. Heat 2 cups of pasteurized heavy cream to 190 degrees, then add 2 tablespoons of lemon juice. Simmer for five minutes, stirring constantly, then remove the pot to cool on the counter for 45 minutes. Strain it in the refrigerator for at least 8 hours, and it will be ready to go.

YOGURT. I make a batch of homemade yogurt just about every week. It takes less than ten minutes of my attention, although it does need at least 8 hours to ferment. You can flavor it or add it to smoothies, and you can strain it to make Greek yogurt if you prefer that texture. This recipe can easily be doubled if you have a lot of yogurt eaters in the house.

Yield: 3 cups   *Prep Time: 10 minutes*
Serving Size: 1 cup   *Ferment Time: 12 hours*

Ingredients:
4 cups whole milk   2 tbsp. plain, whole milk
                                       yogurt

Directions:
1. Heat the milk to a temperature of 180 degrees, and then let it cool to 110 to 115 degrees. You can do this by heating it on the stovetop and monitoring the temperature with a thermometer, or by using a slow cooker. If you use the slow cooker, heat it on low for 2 hours (or until it reaches 180 degrees) and then turn it off and leave it covered in the slow cooker for another 3 hours (or until it cools down to 110 to 115 degrees).
2. Set up a cooler with a thick dish towel inside.
3. Fill a pot with several cups of water, and bring the water to a boil. Place the uncovered pot with the boiling water in the middle of the cooler. Be careful to keep the pot from touching the sides of the cooler (the towel is a buffer). Close the cooler and let it get warm.
4. Pour the milk into a large glass container, and add the yogurt. Stir quickly to combine, then put the top on the container.

5. Place the covered glass container next to the pot of water in the cooler. Ideally, the temperature will be between 90 degrees and 120 degrees. Let the yogurt sit for 4 to 6 hours. After this period, replace the water with a fresh pot of boiling water. Let it sit for another 4 to 6 hours.

6. After 8 to 12 hours, the yogurt should be done. If it hasn't thickened properly, replace the boiling water again and leave it for another 4 hours. There will be liquid on the top (whey) and yogurt at the bottom.

7. Separate the whey for another use by placing the yogurt in a strainer lined with cheesecloth or butter muslin. Let the whey drip out until you have the consistency you want.

8. Store the yogurt in an airtight container in the refrigerator. The whey can be stored separately, and you can use it as a substitute for liquid in baking recipes.

RANCH DRESSING. My children love ranch dressing. After many attempts, I finally came up with a homemade version that they like as much as the store-bought kind. This dressing can be stored for several days in the refrigerator. You can also use it as a dip for veggies or chips.

Yield: 1¼ cup
Serving Size: 2 tablespoons   *Prep Time: 5 minutes*

Ingredients:
½ cup Greek yogurt   ¼ tsp. crushed garlic
½ cup mayonnaise   ½ tsp. salt
¼ cup buttermilk   1 tsp. chopped fresh chives or
2 tsp. lemon juice   other herbs (optional)
½ tsp. onion powder

Directions:
1. Mix all the ingredients together in a small bowl.
2. Take a taste and adjust the seasoning if needed.
3. Use on salad or as a dip for vegetables.

> *"My son said it was the 'awesomest' Ranch ever! High praise indeed." ~Tessa*

Substitution Tip

If you don't have buttermilk on hand, you can make it very easily. Add a tablespoon of white vinegar or lemon juice to a cup of milk and let it sit at room temperature for five minutes. The vinegar will curdle the milk a little, and this mixture is a good substitute for buttermilk.

Baking Necessities

Having a well-stocked pantry is essential. Without the basics on hand, it's difficult to make homemade snacks. This leads to a dependence on pre-packaged snacks, which are more expensive and less nutritious than homemade goodies. Fresh baked food straight from the oven is one of life's simple pleasures.

These homemade baking supplies tend to be less expensive than the store-bought versions. Having them on hand also makes baking go that much more quickly. Pancake mix that's ready to go helps keep things moving when everyone's hungry on a Sunday morning. These recipes are wonderful gifts to give at the holidays too, because there's something extra special about a homemade gift from one kitchen to another.

VANILLA EXTRACT. I love to bake, so I go through a lot of vanilla extract. Those little one- and two-ounce bottles are gone in a flash in my kitchen, though, and I get frustrated by how expensive they are. Vanilla extract costs $.10 per teaspoon at my grocery store. Homemade vanilla extract, on the other hand, costs just $.02 per teaspoon. When I discovered how easy it was to make, I never went back to those little grocery store bottles. Homemade vanilla extract is great to keep on hand to give as a hostess gift as well.

Prep Time: 5 minutes
Steep Time: at least one month

Ingredients:
2 vanilla beans
8 ounces cheap vodka

Directions:
1. Slice the beans open lengthwise and place them in a clean jar. Cover with the vodka, then put a cap on the jar. scrape out half the paste. Use the paste for another
2. Put the jar in a cabinet and forget about it for a month.
3. After a month, open the jar and see if it smells like vanilla or vodka. If it still smells like vodka, put it away for a few more weeks and try again. When you get that nice vanilla extract aroma, you can start using it. The longer it steeps, the stronger vanilla flavor you'll have.

GLUTEN-FREE FLOUR. Most of us eat too much gluten. Before I was diagnosed with a mild gluten sensitivity a few years ago, I ate wheat at breakfast, lunch, and dinner. And snack time. Convenience foods such as cereal, bread, snack bars, and pasta tend to be full of gluten. Some people don't have a problem digesting gluten, but it's still a good idea to eat a varied range of grains rather than depending too heavily on wheat.

Definition: Gluten

Gluten is a substance found in wheat and several other grains. It contributes to the elastic texture of dough. White flour has a high gluten content, while whole wheat flour has a lower gluten content. In gluten-free baking, different flours and starches are mixed together to replicate the texture of wheat flour.

I gave up gluten for a few years, and I needed a gluten-free flour mix that I could keep on hand for baking. The bulk of this mix is brown rice flour, with potato starch and tapioca starch mixed in as well. Although I've returned to eating some whole wheat products, I still keep this mix on hand so I can vary the grains that my family eats. I also like this texture better than whole wheat flour in some recipes.

Ingredients:

5 cups brown rice flour (I like Bob's Red Mill)

2½ cups tapioca flour

1¼ cups potato starch

1½ tbsp. xanthan gum

Directions:

1. Whisk together the ingredients in a large bowl.
2. Transfer the ingredients to an airtight container and store them in a cool, dry cabinet or in the refrigerator.

HOMEMADE PANCAKE MIX. In the groggy haze of morning, it's nice to have homemade pancake mix ready to go so you don't have to think too much while you're still waking up. This simple mix is best stored in the refrigerator or a cool cabinet because whole wheat flour include oils that can shorten its shelf life. If your family is still getting adjusted to whole wheat flour, you can substitute half of it with unbleached, all-purpose flour while you're making the transition.

Ingredients:

5 cups white whole wheat flour

5 tsp. baking soda

5 tsp. salt

½ cup sugar (optional)

Directions:

1. Whisk together the ingredients in a large bowl.
2. Transfer the ingredients to an airtight container and store them in a cool, dry cabinet or in the refrigerator.
3. To make 12 pancakes, stir together the following in a large bowl: 3 eggs, 1 ¼ cup plain yogurt or milk, and 1 ½ cup pancake mix. Stir together until just combined, and make the pancakes on a hot griddle.

PUMPKIN PIE SPICE. Every year, I go a little pumpkin crazy from September to November. I make pumpkin bread, pumpkin cookies, pumpkin cake (p. 208), pumpkin pie, and even pumpkin ice cream (page 221). I actually never get tired of it, but I give my family a break once winter hits. These pumpkin recipes can be made even more quickly when I have some pumpkin pie spice ready to go. I like to store it in a little 4-ounce mason jar.

Ingredients:

2 tbsp. cinnamon

2 tsp. ginger

2 tsp. nutmeg

1 tsp. allspice

Directions:

1. In a small bowl, stir together all the ingredients.
2. Store in an airtight container for as long as you would store the individual spices, typically one year.

Fast Food Alternatives

Fast food is such a tempting option at meal time. From tacos to pizza to chicken, there are loads of options at cheap prices. But you get what you pay for, and fast food restaurants typically use low-quality ingredients that don't nourish you. I know this from watching documentaries and looking at ingredient lists online. But more importantly, I know this because of how I feel after I eat food from one of these places. Stomach troubles, low energy, and poor sleep remind me that homemade food is better.

There are many Mexican fast-food chains, but homemade tacos can be a fun family dinner at home (page 160). I occasionally raise the white flag and order pizza for my family, but I typically make it myself because it's so easy. Again, there's nothing wrong with ordering out on occasion, but ideally this is the exception rather than the rule. And when you do it, at least you know that it's not the only way to get pizza on your table.

This homemade taco seasoning is a wonderful topping for beans or meat in your Taco Night spread.

TACO SEASONING. We love taco night in our house (p. 160). It's the perfect dinner for people with different tastes because everyone chooses the fillings they want. To season the beans and the meat, I use this recipe. Store-bought taco seasoning typically includes ingredients like maltodextrin, partially hydrogenated soybean oil, and silicon dioxide. These are not ingredients I want to feed my family, so I'm happy to have a healthy version of homemade taco seasoning. This seasoning also makes a delicious topping for popcorn (p. 113).

Yield: 5 tablespoons
Prep Time: 5 minutes

Ingredients:

2 tbsp. chili powder

4 tsp. salt

2 tsp. cumin

1 tsp. onion powder

1 tsp. smoked paprika

½ tsp. oregano

½ tsp. black pepper

Directions:

1. In a small bowl, stir together all the ingredients.
2. Season taco meat or beans with the mixture to taste. I use about 2 teaspoons to season a half pound of meat.
3. Store in an airtight container for as long as you would store the individual spices, typically up to a year.

ENCHILADA SAUCE. Homemade enchilada sauce is one of the easiest condiments to make. It takes just a few minutes to put together, and it tastes fantastic. If you like it spicier, you can add some diced jalapeno pepper with the onion. Freeze the extra sauce and save it for a Mexican meal on a busy night.

Yield: 2 cups

Prep time: 5 minutes
Cook time: 15 minutes

Ingredients:

1 tbsp. olive oil

¼ cup diced onion

1 clove garlic, crushed

2 tbsp. chili powder

1½ tsp. cumin

1 tsp. salt

2 cups tomato sauce

Directions:

1. In a medium skillet, cook the onion in the olive oil over medium-low heat for five minutes, or until soft. Add the crushed garlic, chili powder, cumin, and salt to the pan. Stir and cook for another minute to combine the flavors.
2. Add the tomato sauce to the pan. Simmer gently for 10 minutes, stirring occasionally.
3. Let the sauce cool, then transfer it to an airtight container. You can store it in the refrigerator for several days, or freeze it for several months.

BARBECUE SAUCE. Barbecue sauce is a delicious topping for plain cooked chicken. I like to keep a batch in the freezer so I can make barbecue chicken any time. By making your own barbecue sauce, you can avoid all the refined sugar and other questionable ingredients the store-bought versions typically contain.

Yield: 1¼ cups

Prep Time: 10 minutes
Cook Time: 30 minutes

Ingredients:

1 tbsp. olive oil
¾ cup minced onion
1 clove garlic, crushed
1 tbsp. soy sauce
1 cup tomato sauce
1 tsp. cumin

½ tsp. dry mustard
½ tsp. smoked paprika
¼ cup apple cider vinegar (or other vinegar)
3 tbsp. honey

Directions:

1. In a medium saucepan over medium-low heat, sauté the onion in the olive oil until softened, about 5 minutes.

2. Add the crushed garlic and cook for another minute. I use a microplane to turn the garlic into a purée so I don't end up with little chunks of garlic in the sauce.

3. Add the remaining ingredients. Stir together, and simmer over low heat until thickened (about 20 minutes). If you want a smooth sauce without any chunks of onion, you can purée it with an immersion blender or food processor.

4. Store this in the refrigerator for several days, or freeze it for several months.

PIZZA. Before my family transitioned to a whole foods diet, we used to order pizza all the time. I know we weren't alone. According to the National Association of Pizza Operators, approximately 3 billion pizzas are sold in the United States each year. Pizza makes a quick, easy, inexpensive meal. I still order pizza on occasion, but I prefer to make it myself most of the time.

The dough and sauce are simple to make, and the sky's the limit when it comes to toppings. I love this easy sauce recipe, but you can also use marinara sauce (p. 166). Make the dough and sauce ahead of time and freeze them if you have a busy night coming up later in the week. Defrost them in the refrigerator a day before you need them. On baking day, place the dough on the counter in an airtight container so it can come to room temperature.

Yield: 2 large pizzas
Serving Size: 2 slices

Prep Time: 15 minutes, plus
30 minute rise time
Cook Time: 10 minutes

Dough Ingredients:
1 cup warm water
1½ tsp. active dry yeast
2 tsp. sugar
3 tbsp. olive oil

3 cups white whole wheat flour
¾ teaspoon salt

Sauce Ingredients:

2 cups tomato sauce | ¼ tsp. salt
½ tsp. oregano | 1 tsp. red wine vinegar
½ tsp. sugar | ¼ tsp. onion powder

Directions:

1. To make the crust, mix together the warm water, yeast, and sugar. Let it sit for 5 minutes, then add the oil.
2. In the bowl of a stand mixer, mix together the flour and the salt. Add the wet ingredients.
3. With a dough hook, beat the mixture until a ball of dough forms. The dough should be well hydrated but not sticky. (It should be almost sticky.) If it's sticky, add a little more flour. If it seems too dry, add a little more water.
4. Divide the dough into two balls. Cover the dough with plastic wrap and let it rise for 30 minutes.
5. While the dough is rising, prepare the sauce. Stir together the sauce ingredients in a medium saucepan, and simmer for 5 minutes to cook off some of the liquid.
6. Preheat the oven to 425 degrees and grease 2 baking sheets. Alternately, you can cook these pizzas on baking stones.
7. Roll out each piece of dough into a circle ¼-inch to 1/2-inch thick and place them on the cookie sheets. Top the dough with the sauce, followed by cheese and any other toppings you'd like.
8. Bake for 8 to 10 minutes, until the cheese is melted and beginning to turn brown. If you overcook it, the crust will be dry.

Variation:

Instead of making pizza, you can turn this recipe into calzones. At Step 7, place the sauce, cheese, and other topping on half of the dough circle. Then fold the other half over the toppings and press down the edges to seal in the fillings. Pierce the calzones a few times with a fork, and bake at 425 degrees for about 15 minutes, or until the dough begins to turn light brown. These can be eaten right away or frozen for a quick dinner on another night.

By learning how to make the recipes in this book, you'll gain the skills needed to master the art of feeding your family real food. You won't be bound to take-out and packaged foods, and you'll have so many options when it comes time to eat. Food cooked from scratch brings something special to a home. I wish your family great health and joy as you learn to conquer your kitchen!

Appendix One
Basic Cooking Terms

Bake: Cook in the oven at a specified temperature.

Boil: Heat water to a temperature of 212 degrees Fahrenheit. The liquid will get hot enough for large, rolling bubbles to break the surface.

Broil: Cook briefly under direct heat in the oven.

Chop: Cut into bite-sized pieces.

Dice: Cut into very small pieces.

Fold: Gently combine and aerate two or more ingredients using a bottom-to-top "folding" motion with a large spoon or spatula.

Knead: Work dough with the heels of your hands in a pressing and folding motion until it becomes smooth and uniform.

Marinate: Submerge food in a seasoned liquid to infuse flavor into the food before cooking.

Mince: Cut into tiny pieces, as small as possible when cutting with a knife.

Parboil/Blanch: Cook food briefly in boiling water to lock in nutrients, flavor, and color.

Purée: Blend food until it has a smooth texture.

Sauté: Cook quickly on the stovetop in oil or butter.

Simmer: Cook in liquid over a near boil so that bubbles are just barely breaking the surface.

Appendix Two
Kitchen Measurement Conversion Chart

This handy chart will help you to convert recipe quantities from one unit of measurement to another. Sometimes it's easier to think in terms of cups rather than pints or quarts or gallons. Refer to this chart to see how different quantities measure up.

KITCHEN MEASUREMENT
CONVERSION CHART

1 tbs.	=	3 tsp.
2 tbs.	=	⅛ cup
4 tbs.	=	¼ cup
6 tbs.	=	⅛ cup
8 tbs.	=	½ cup
12 tbs.	=	¾ cup
16 tbs.	=	1 cup
48 tsp	=	1 cup
8 fluid ounces	=	1 cup
1 pint	=	2 cups
1 quart	=	2 pints
1 quart	=	4 cups
1 gallon	=	4 quarts
1 gallon	=	16 cups
1 pound	=	16 ounces

Appendix Three
"Dirty Dozen" and "Clean Fifteen" Produce Guide

It's better to eat lots of fruits and vegetables than it is to avoid them out of fear of pesticide exposure. However, this fear is a valid one, and many people are looking for guidelines about which produce is best to buy organic. Each year, the Environmental Working Group evaluates the amount of pesticide residue found on produce sold at grocery stores.

If you don't want to buy all organic produce but you'd like to minimize your pesticide exposure, the EWG recommends purchasing the organic version of the items on the "Dirty Dozen" list. Conventionally grown items on the "Clean Fifteen" list contain smaller amounts of pesticides, so these are considered safer to buy in non-organic form.

The Environmental Working Group updates these ratings once a year, and this is the 2014 version. For the most updated version you can check http://www.ewg.org/foodnews/list.php.

The Environmental Working Group also notes that kale, collard greens, and summer squash have traces of exceptionally risky pesticides, so they recommend buying the organic version of these items, too.

For the full list of 48 items evaluated, visit the Environmental Working Group: http://www.ewg.org/foodnews/list.php
You can even download an app for your smart phone to keep track of the list while you're at the store.

DIRTY AND CLEAN

(Note: You can always download the latest version at
http://ConqueringYourKitchen.com)

DIRTY DOZEN

Apples
Celery
Cherry Tomatoes
Cucumbers
Grapes
Hot Peppers
Imported Nectarines
Peaches
Potatoes
Spinach
Strawberries
Sweet bell peppers

CLEAN FIFTEEN

Asparagus
Avocado
Cabbage
Canteloupe
Corn
Eggplant
Grapefruit
Kiwi
Mangos
Mushrooms
Onions
Papayas
Pineapples
Sweet Peas
Sweet Potatoes

Appendix Four
Where to Store Produce

Some produce does best stored in the refrigerator, while other produce should be stored at room temperature on the counter or in a drawer. The crisper drawers at the bottom of the refrigerator have more humidity than the rest of the fridge, and they keep most refrigerated produce fresher than the dry main compartment would. As fruits and vegetables ripen, some of them give off ethylene gas, which can bother other produce. For this reason, it's generally best to keep fruit in one drawer and vegetables in the other drawer.

Once the fruits on the "room temperature" list have ripened, they can be placed in the refrigerator for a couple days if you're not ready to eat them right away.

WHERE TO STORE
PRODUCE CHECKLIST

REFRIGERATOR	ROOM TEMPERATURE
Apples	Avocados
Asparagus	Bananas
Beets	Garlic
Bell Peppers	Mangoes
Berries	Melons
Broccoli/Brussels Sprouts	Nectarines
Cabbage	Onions
Carrots	Peaches
Cauliflower	Pears
Celery	Pineapples
Cherries	Plums
Corn	Potatoes
Cucumbers	Sweet Potatoes
Eggplant	Tomatoes
Ginger	Winter Squash
Grapes	
Green Beans	
Greens and Herbs	
Kiwi	
Leeks	
Lemons/Limes/Oranges	
Pomegranates	
Radishes	
Rhubarb	
Scallions	
Summer Squash	
Tomatillos	
Turnips	

Appendix Five
Other Resources

There are many books, movies, and websites that teach about the shortcomings of the processed food system. There are also quite a few wonderful resources to help you with all aspects of conquering your kitchen, including food philosophy, kitchen organization, meal planning, shopping, and cooking.

Books:
Food Matters by Mark Bittman
How to Cook Everything by Mark Bittman
The Omnivore's Dilemma by Michael Pollan
In Defense of Food by Michael Pollan
Fast Food Nation by Eric Schlosser
Joy of Cooking by Irma Rombauer, Marion Rombauer Becker, and Ethan Becker
Moosewood Restaurant cookbooks by Mollie Katzen

Movies and Television:
Fed Up
Food Inc.
Supersize Me
Genetic Roulette
Diet for a New America
Jamie Oliver's Food Revolution

Websites:
www.thefresh20.com
www.plantoeat.com
www.localharvest.org
www.eatlocalgrown.org
www.organicdeals.com
www.eatwild.com

Appendix Six
Make-Ahead Meals

Preparing your meals ahead of time can be an amazing way to save time and streamline meal preparation. These recipes are all meals that you can make ahead for busy days. Also check out the sidebar on page 48 for freezer-friendly meals.

Apple Pie Oatmeal – page 76
Blueberry-Banana Baked Oatmeal – page 77
Maple Granola – page 78
Boiled Eggs – page 83
Waffles – page 91
French Toast Casserole – page 94
Kale Chips – page 131
Baked Potatoes – page 136
Basil Pesto - page145
Pasta Casserole – page 167
Whole Chicken – page 173
Quinoa Salad – page 187
Blueberry Peach Crisp - page 192
Apple Pie – page 195
All Snacks (Chapter begins page 102)
All of the Soups (Section begins page 147)
Fresh From the Oven Desserts (Section begins page 203)

ABOUT THE AUTHOR

Annemarie Rossi is a mother who got tired of feeding her family processed food. Raised in a Twinkie-loving household, she somehow always had an affinity for vegetables too. When she set out to learn how to cook and find healthy food that her young children would enjoy, it opened up a new way of life for her.

Inspired by food experts like Mark Bittman, Jamie Oliver, and Michael Pollan, Annemarie embraced the idea of feeding her family nothing but real food. Their diet became focused on whole grains, fresh produce, varied protein sources, and lots of healthy, homemade snacks and desserts. She learned that she could make her own yogurt, cheese, PopTarts, and pizza dough. Her versions didn't have the chemical additives that the store-bought versions typically had. Her kitchen became a science lab, and the family enjoyed many taste tests. Even the messy failures tasted pretty good.

With the support of her husband and children, Annemarie has made this approach to food a way of life for her family. She's not a nutritionist or a professional cook. She's just a regular mom trying to do the right thing for her family. In order to share what she's learned with others, Annemarie founded Real Food Real Deals.

This food blog helps people to eat a whole foods diet while sticking to a budget. The website features hundreds of affordable, tasty recipes made with real food ingredients. A math person at heart, Annemarie does price breakdowns for all her recipes. People often complain that eating healthy is too expensive, but she shows that this isn't the case for many different types of recipes.

Annemarie received her undergraduate degree in Psychology from the College of the Holy Cross, as well as a Master's Degree in Pastoral Ministry from Boston College. Now a suburban mom in the Boston area, Annemarie has been happy to see a trend in healthier eating throughout New England. She enjoys traveling with her family, and they always visit farmers' markets and restaurants that celebrate locally sourced food while on vacation. To keep up to date with Annemarie's recipes, tips, and food travel stories, follow her at www.realfoodrealdeals.com.

ABOUT UNTRAINED HOUSEWIFE GUIDES

The Untrained Housewife Guides are an extension of the website, http://untrainedhousewife.com, which seeks to empower people to take the next step in their quest for intentional and self-sufficient living. Living intentionally can take many forms and we are actively seeking unique and encouraging voices to help create in-depth books on a variety of topics for the community.

GETTING PREPARED – Available on Amazon and other book retailers. Getting Prepared is a beginner's manual for how to get started feeling more confident and self-reliant during life's unexpected happenings. While we all certainly hope that nothing bad will ever happen, we all secretly know that it could. From emergency grab-and-go bags to a 30-day food plan, this book will walk you through all the elements to consider. You'll find words of wisdom from someone who's done it all and can guide you step-by-step without overwhelming you. If you've thought about trying to get better prepared and developing an emergency plan, but have been unsure about where to start, this is the book for you!

Home Business Victory – Coming Soon! A guide for everything you need to know to start a successful home-based business. By Karis Bellisario

Learn more about coming titles and how to submit a manuscript idea at http://angelaenglandmedia.com/.

23958885R00153

Made in the USA
San Bernardino, CA
06 September 2015